Early praise for *React for Real*

This book does a remarkable job of illuminating the concepts of React using easy-to-follow examples. A must-read for novice or mid-level developers interested in using React in a professional software development environment.

➤ **Wolfert de Kraker**
Software Developer, Stager

React for Real is a great way to get started with React, with clear explanations and examples that get you a lot further than a short tutorial. Recommended.

➤ **Peter Hilton**
Independent Software Developer, Co-Author of *Play for Scala*

A pragmatic and focused introduction to React, this book will equip you with a great foundation to enjoy and be productive with React.

➤ **Johan Marais**
Senior Developer

I recommend this book to people who want to learn React from scratch, because it explains the concepts concisely and from the ground up.

➤ **Giorgio Mandolini**
Web and Mobile Developer, e-xtrategy

This concise and pragmatic book focuses on the essentials of the React ecosystem, including Redux, and helps you understand and explore React with confidence.

➤ **Suresh Iyer**
Polyglot Programmer and Senior Staff Applications Engineer, ServiceNow

In just about 100 pages, this book contains all the essential details you'll need to start building real-world React apps. It also addresses some of the challenges in the React community, including using React with non-React libraries, proper ways to manage state, and how to test components.

➤ **Justice Mba**
Front-End Engineer, VConnect

React for Real

Front-End Code, Untangled

Ludovico Fischer

The Pragmatic Bookshelf

Raleigh, North Carolina

Many of the designations used by manufacturers and sellers to distinguish their products are claimed as trademarks. Where those designations appear in this book, and The Pragmatic Programmers, LLC was aware of a trademark claim, the designations have been printed in initial capital letters or in all capitals. The Pragmatic Starter Kit, The Pragmatic Programmer, Pragmatic Programming, Pragmatic Bookshelf, PragProg and the linking *g* device are trademarks of The Pragmatic Programmers, LLC.

Every precaution was taken in the preparation of this book. However, the publisher assumes no responsibility for errors or omissions, or for damages that may result from the use of information (including program listings) contained herein.

Our Pragmatic books, screencasts, and audio books can help you and your team create better software and have more fun. Visit us at *https://pragprog.com*.

The team that produced this book includes:

Publisher: Andy Hunt
VP of Operations: Janet Furlow
Development Editor: Brian P. Hogan
Copy Editor: Nicole Abramowtiz
Layout: Gilson Graphics

For sales, volume licensing, and support, please contact *support@pragprog.com*.

For international rights, please contact *rights@pragprog.com*.

Printed in the United States of America.
ISBN-13: 978-1-68050-263-3
Printed on acid-free paper.
Book version: P1.0—August 2017

Contents

Acknowledgments

I would like to thank my editors, Brian Hogan and Susannah Pfalzer, as well as the technical reviewers: Giovanni Asproni, Allan Chaplin, Nicolai de Guzman, Suresh Iyer, Giorgio Mandolini, Artem Sapegin, Francesco Strazzullo, and Allen Wyma.

A special thank you to Mark Erikson for his suggestions concerning Redux, and to Peter Hilton for his impromptu technical review.

I would also like to thank everyone with whom I have discussed this project and who has encouraged me along the way, including my parents, Aunt Josette and Uncle Giorgio, Giuditta, Marcello, Mike, Min, Nicolas, Stefano from Amsterdam, Stefano from Brussels, Sylvie, Tata, Thomas, Tingxiang, Valerio, Wolfert and Xiaoxia.

Preface

Many web applications allow users to browse and edit content without reloading the page—for example, editing a document, selecting people to email from a contact list, or even browsing a list of events and buying a ticket. While web pages used to be just about the display of information, now a fair amount of business logic might run in the browser. To handle this logic, you often create specialized code—the data model for your application.

In all these applications, you must update the user interface and data model consistently. Since every web page is a tree of elements, called the DOM, you could apply a change directly to the DOM on every action, but this makes it difficult to distinguish business logic from visual adjustments. When you make visual adjustments, you manipulate DOM elements to change the appearance of the user interface. That's why web developers have started to prefer to store the data in a separate data structure, like a JavaScript object. But now you have a new problem: you need to communicate the changes from the data structure to the DOM and back.

You could add DOM elements with native browser functions such as appendChild() and change element contents by overwriting the innerHTML attribute on DOM nodes. This forces you to spend time on boilerplate code, away from your application's core logic. Since this boilerplate turns out similarly across different web applications, it makes sense to offload DOM manipulation to a library.

React is a JavaScript library that automatically updates the DOM when the data changes. It makes writing highly interactive web pages faster and more reliable. It's easy to use and integrates with a wealth of techniques and other libraries.

In this book, you'll learn the fundamentals of building user interfaces with React and how to prepare an application for production so that it loads efficiently. You'll also test components, use React with the Redux library for more complex applications, and work with other libraries. You'll get hands-on practice as you work through complete examples.

Who Should Read This Book

If you already have some web development experience in languages like PHP, JavaScript, Ruby, or Java, and would like to learn React, this is the book for you. It's not necessary that you have front-end web development experience, although you should be familiar with HTML. You can use a number of languages to write front-end code. In this book, we use JavaScript, as it's the most used language in the browser. We'll explain novel JavaScript concepts as we go along.

What's in This Book

This book introduces you to the fundamentals of React and teaches you strategies to build applications, starting from the basics and building up to more advanced cases. Once you've completed this book, you can learn more online through tutorials or other books.

The book focuses on applications that run inside a web browser. It uses hands-on examples to get you started from basic building blocks, to more advanced architectures. We'll cover building the application, testing, and integrating with other libraries.

In Chapter 1, *An Introduction to Components*, on page 1, you'll create React components to build your first application using functions, classes, and JSX.

In Chapter 2, *Work with State and Events*, on page 17, you'll make your application respond to input and make calls to a web server.

Chapter 3, *Create a Production Build*, on page 31 shows you how to create an optimized build so that your application loads quickly in production. It also introduces modules to help you handle large code bases.

You'll test business logic as well as user interface behavior in Chapter 4, *Test Your React Components*, on page 49, as you explore different techniques to test your React applications.

Sometimes you'll need to create more complex applications where different components all interact with the same data. In Chapter 5, *Using Redux as a Central Data Store*, on page 63, you'll use Redux, a library to handle applications where React's basic model can become inadequate.

Finally, not all JavaScript code out there plays well with React's automatic DOM updates. In Chapter 6, *Work Well with Others*, on page 85, you'll integrate React with libraries that have conflicting mechanisms.

Although you can use React to render applications on the server, we won't cover that in this book, as it is a rapidly evolving area, and competing solutions depend on the web framework you use server-side. We won't cover using React to write native applications for iOS and Android either.

What You Need

You'll need a computer running Windows 10 or a recent version of Linux or macOS, with a recent release of either the Chrome or Firefox web browser. The code you'll write will work in all recent browsers, but sometimes I'll suggest you install some developer tools, which only work in Chrome and Firefox, to inspect the application while it's running. You'll need to be able to install software on your computer, and you'll need an Internet connection.

You'll need a text editor or an IDE. If you're unsure what to pick, Visual Studio Code[1] supports React well. You'll also need to use a terminal to type in commands.

Conventions

When you'll have to type a command in the command prompt or terminal, it will look like this:

```
$ npm
```

The dollar sign represents the terminal prompt. It's there to tell you that you should type the code in your terminal, but you should just type whatever comes after the dollar sign, without the dollar sign itself.

Other times, you'll see code snippets. The file name above the code sample tells you where to find the file in the book's source code download.

If you read the electronic version of the book, clicking the file name above the code lets you see the full source for that file on the Pragmatic Bookshelf web site.

Where to Go for Help

You can ask questions and provide feedback in the book's forum linked on the Pragmatic Bookshelf page for this book.[2] On the same page, you'll find links to download the source code for the book's examples and to the errata.

Let's start by learning about React's basic building block, components.

---

1. https://code.visualstudio.com/
2. https://pragprog.com/book/lfreact/

CHAPTER 1

An Introduction to Components

React helps you build dynamic web applications by automatically updating the DOM when your data model changes. On top of updating the DOM, React lets you iterate on the interface by combining, expanding, and moving around self-contained elements, until you've hit the right design. These self-contained elements are called *components*.

Every application contains buttons, text inputs, labels, legends, and so on. Instead of building the user interface from single HTML elements like <div> or <p>, and manipulating these elements one at a time when you need to apply some changes, you first group single elements into components. Then you build the whole page by combining the components. Components are like custom elements that precisely match your application's functionality. Instead of manipulating HTML elements one by one to update the interface, you pass new data to the components, and React takes care of tedious manipulations. To be able to use components, you'll define your interface mostly in JavaScript.

React enforces strict rules to share data between components, which we'll explore in this chapter and the next. While you develop and debug, this helps you trace the source of the data that's displayed.

Since it gets rid of code that manipulates HTML elements, React lets you focus on the logic behind the application—the model of the application. React lets you use any data structure you want in your model. You can use a lot of different libraries with React, so you can scale the complexity depending on the task at hand.

In this first chapter, you'll learn how to map data to HTML elements. You'll learn a few basic React concepts such as *renderers*, *components*, and *props*. Then you'll build a text box with a counter that displays the word count automatically.

Set Up Your First Project

When you build a React app, you create a description of the desired result, then hand it over to React, which takes charge of modifying the DOM to match your description. Instead of enhancing existing HTML, you define the whole HTML structure in JavaScript. This makes it simpler to express the UI as a function of the data.

We'll test our setup by outputting an <h1> header with the "Hello World" message. Typically, you use React to insert components into an existing HTML page, so you'll usually generate the basic structure like the <head> and <body> tags on the server. You'll use two files: index.html, which will contain the basic HTML skeleton, and hello.js, which will hold all the JavaScript code.

```
├── index.html
├── hello.js
```

Create a basic HTML skeleton in index.html that looks like the following:

```
intro/index.html
<!DOCTYPE html>
<html>
  <head>
    <meta charset="utf-8"/>
    <meta name="viewport" content="width=device-width, initial-scale=1"/>
    <title>Hello World</title>
  </head>
  <body>
    <div id="app"></div>
  </body>
</html>
```

The fastest way to run React code is to include the React and ReactDOM libraries from a Content Delivery Network, or CDN, using <script> tags. Insert the CDN links above the closing <body> tag. You'll load React before your own code, which you also include with a <script> tag:

```
intro/index.html
➤    <script src="https://unpkg.com/react@15/dist/react.js"></script>
➤    <script src="https://unpkg.com/react-dom@15/dist/react-dom.js"></script>
➤    <script src="hello.js"></script>
</body>
```

We're linking to the development builds of React and ReactDOM. To get more helpful error messages, use the development build of React and ReactDOM, which run much slower than the production builds; in production, link to the production builds of React you find on the React website.[1]

You'll render "Hello World" in an <h1> tag inside the <div> with the *app* id=. To do this, create a React element, which is a JavaScript description of a DOM structure that React uses to efficiently render interfaces. Open hello.js in your favorite text editor and type this code:

```
intro/hello.js
ReactDOM.render(
  React.createElement('h1', {}, 'Hello World!'),
  document.getElementById('app')
);
```

Let's break down the code. ReactDOM.render() takes a description of the UI and creates the matching DOM elements. React.createElement() returns a description of the UI. The first argument to React.createElement() determines the top element. Passing a string, 'h1', returns a representation of the matching HTML tag, <h1>. The second argument configures additional properties of the top element—for example, HTML attributes. Pass an empty object since we don't need to configure anything. Each argument after that becomes a child element of the top element. In this case, <h1> has a single child, the "Hello world" text.

ReactDOM.render() creates a new tree of DOM nodes that matches the description returned by React.createElement(). It places the result inside the DOM node you pass as its second argument. document.getElementById() is a native browser API that takes a string and retrieves the DOM node with a matching id=.

Save hello.js. Then open index.html in your browser, and "Hello World" appears in all its glory:

Hello World!

If you don't see anything, make sure the element with id="app" exists, and that you've saved your HTML and your JavaScript files.

You've seen how to describe HTML elements with React.createElement(). Next, we'll use this ability to create configurable interface elements.

---

1. https://facebook.github.io/react/

Create a Component

Components are JavaScript functions or classes that accept parameters, called *props*, and return a description of the UI based on those parameters. In this way, you can render the HTML elements and the application data in one go, without writing additional code to update values inside the HTML. When the data changes, you pass updated props to the component. React takes care of re-rendering the page.

A component can be any JavaScript function that takes an object as a parameter and returns an element created with React.createElement(). Since components are JavaScript functions, you can transform the data with the full power of JavaScript before creating the output. Our first component will be a function that takes two numbers and displays the sum. We'll call this function Adder(). Define Adder() in a new file named Adder.js.

```
intro/Adder.js
function Adder({ n1, n2 }) {
  const sum = n1 + n2;
  return React.createElement('h1', {}, sum);
}
```

Adder() takes a JavaScript object and returns a React element. Returning a React element makes Adder() a component. When you define an object parameter for a component function, the object properties automatically become props. The object parameter has two properties, n1 and n2, which represent the numbers to add. When you use this syntax, JavaScript automatically assigns the value of the parameter properties to variables with the same name in the function body, so the n1 and n2 automatically take the values of the n1 and n2 properties. We add n1 and n2 and assign the result to sum. We then return a React element describing an <h1> header containing the sum.

Declaring values with const prevents you from accidentally overwriting them later, as JavaScript throws an error if you attempt to reassign them. It might sound surprising, but outside of loops, it's fairly rare that you need to assign a new value to the same variable. If you do, declare the variable with let. let will stand out outside of a loop, and you will know that something special is going on. If you've used JavaScript in the past, you might be used to declaring variables with var. The advantage of let compared to var is that the scope of the let variable is the same as const variables, while var variables follow different scoping rules.

Next, we'll create a React element based on our component, then render the React element to the DOM.

To set prop values, pass an object with properties matching those in the component function parameter as the second argument to React.createElement(). For example, set n1 to 2, and n2 to 4. Then pass the result of React.createElement() to ReactDOM.render() to render it to the DOM. Add the call to ReactDOM.render() below the Adder() definition in Adder.js:

```
intro/Adder.js
ReactDOM.render(
  React.createElement(Adder, { n1: 2, n2: 4 }),
  document.getElementById('app')
);
```

Include Adder.js in index.html instead of hello.js and reload the page. You'll see the sum of 2 and 4 appear.

If you use either Chrome or Firefox, the React developer tools browser extension[2] offers a great way to debug your component. In Chrome or Firefox, go to the add-ons or extensions settings, search for "React developer tools," and install the extension. Once you've installed the extension, activate the developer console. You'll notice a new tab labeled React. Expanding the React tab reveals two panes:

If the extension doesn't work, try checking "Allow access to file URLs" in the extension options page.

The left pane displays the component hierarchy on the current page and lets you expand and select components. The right pane displays the props for the selected components. First, check that the developer tools detect the Adder component. If not, look in the console for error messages. The application might have failed to start at all. Then, select the Adder component and check that the n1 and n2 match the numbers that you passed.

A React component can receive props, perform computations, and describe how to display the result. The next step is to create more complex structures by combining multiple React elements. Since React.createElement() calls can become difficult to read, we can use an alternative syntax called JSX to create components.

---

2.   github.com/facebook/react-devtools

Describe Elements with JSX

JSX is an alternative syntax for React.createElement() that doesn't introduce any new functionality, but makes the code easier to read.

You may be used to describing the user interface in separate template files. React developers came up with an unorthodox solution: a new syntax to describe user interfaces inside JavaScript files. Instead of writing React.createElement() by hand, you write the element description in a syntax that's almost identical to HTML, called JSX. Then, before the application runs, you process your source with a tool called Babel to replace JSX with React.createElement().

When compared to templates, the advantage to this approach is that there are fewer special rules to learn than with a separate template language, and error messages tend to be easier to interpret. The trade-off is that you need a build step to prepare your code for production. To get started fast, right now we'll use an in-browser Babel transform: it's too slow for production use and may sometimes lead to odd runtime errors, but it's enough to practice the syntax.

Let's convert our Adder component to use JSX instead of React.createElement(). Modify your code so it looks like this:

intro/Adder.js
```
function Adder({ n1, n2 }) {
  const sum = n1 + n2;
  return <h1>{sum}</h1>;
}
```

In this version, we return an <h1> element, as if we'd written it in HTML. We then output the value of the sum inside the <h1> element by surrounding the variable name with braces. You can mix the result of any JavaScript expression into the generated markup by enclosing the JavaScript expression in braces.

Once you convert Adder to JSX, the application won't work anymore because the browser can't interpret JSX. We'll use the Babel standalone transformer to translate on the fly JSX into React.createElement() calls. Open index.html. Insert a link to Babel's standalone transpiler right above your own code, and then change your code's type= to *text/babel*:

intro/index-jsx.html
```
<script src="https://unpkg.com/react@15/dist/react.js"></script>
<script src="https://unpkg.com/react-dom@15/dist/react-dom.js"></script>
<script src="https://unpkg.com/babel-standalone@6/babel.min.js"></script>
<script type="text/babel" src="Adder.js"></script>
```

In Chrome, Babel standalone doesn't work if you open index.html as a local file. You need to serve index.html from a local web server. A solution that works on every platform where Chrome runs is to install the Web Server for Chrome extension.[3] After installing the extension in Chrome, select the directory containing index.html as the directory to serve and navigate to the URL displayed by the Web Server extension.

Open index.html in your browser, and the text displays again. If something doesn't work, check that you included Babel before your own code and that you've changed the type= attribute to "text/babel" on the <script> tag for your own code; otherwise, Babel won't convert it.

Now that everything is back into working order, let's also use JSX in React-DOM.render(). Convert the React.createElement() call inside ReactDOM.render().

Enclose the component name in angle brackets, as if it were a custom HTML element. Capitalize component names, or else React will try to create them directly in the DOM, even if no HTML element with that name exists. Set the prop values as if they were HTML attributes, but surround each prop with braces instead of quotes to prevent React from interpreting them as strings instead of numbers. Your code should look like the following:

```
intro/Adder.js
ReactDOM.render(<Adder n1={2} n2={4} />, document.getElementById('app'));
```

You'll use JSX for the rest of the book. The in-browser conversion runs too slowly for production apps, so in Chapter 3, *Create a Production Build*, on page 31, you'll convert your source code to valid JavaScript before deploying the application. For now, we'll use the in-browser transform so you can keep focusing on React.

Let's review all we learned so far. React.createElement() generates a description of the UI. It can use either strings or a component. Strings describe single HTML elements. Components combine multiple elements and describe a piece of UI as a function of data. It is like a pipe that swallows data and outputs a representation of the UI:

```
Data --> Component --> Element
```

React.createElement() accepts either a string that defines plain HTML elements, or a component. By passing a component to React.createElement(), you can combine components into more complex elements until you've built the whole interface. You can replace React.createElement() with JSX. Even though JSX looks

---

3. https://chrome.google.com/webstore/detail/web-server-for-chrome/ofhbbkphhbklhfoeikjpcbhemlocgigb

like HTML, Babel eventually converts everything to React.createElement() calls. Babel assumes elements that start with a lowercase define regular HTML elements, and elements that start with a capital are based on components.

ReactDOM.render() takes this description of the UI and constructs the actual DOM nodes:

```
Element --> Renderer --> UI
```

React then ensures that the interface stays up to date as the data in props changes.

Now that we've got the basics down, we can build more complex applications.

Match Components and Data

Let's put all of this new knowledge to use by creating something more concrete. We'll build a word counter widget that takes some text and a target word count and displays the word count and a progress bar. In Chapter 2, *Work with State and Events*, on page 17, we'll learn how to update the text and the word count as the user types, but first, we'll set up the word counter with a fixed text. When we're done, our component will look like this:

Enter your text:

Word count: 0

Progress

In most applications, we don't operate on a jumble of disconnected data; there are relationships between the data we work on. For example, the count and the progress bar are both based on the text. There are also relationships between UI elements, as user interface elements that display related data are often grouped together. We can take advantage of this fact to map the data to the user interface.

Let components mirror the relationships within the data. One component will perform the calculations, then use props to pass the results of the calculation to its children. Since components only receive data from their parents, it's easier to trace where the data is coming from to debug the application.

This word counter is so simple, you could probably write it without any libraries, but it's a great example because it will give you a feel for how to organize the component structure based on the data you need to display. To get started, let's look at the relationships within the data. In this diagram, the arrows go from data to other data that derives from it:

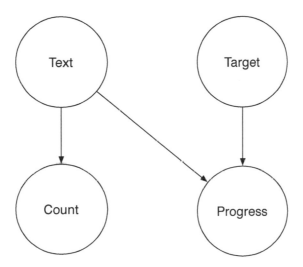

The text and target word count are defined when you create the component. The count derives from the text, and the progress derives from the text and the target word count.

We could make one component that outputs the text box, the counter, and the progress bar, but it's better to create these as separate components. In a larger application, small, focused components make it easier to understand what each component does, and it then becomes easier to refactor the application and move components around.

Spreading the application logic across many components makes it harder to follow, so we'll try to keep it together. Instead of passing the text and the target to every component, we'll calculate the count and progress in a *container* component higher up in the hierarchy. Then we'll pass them as props to *presentational* components down the hierarchy.

Container components contain logic and perform calculations. Presentational components just display the props. Since props pass from parents to children, you must place smart components higher up in the hierarchy. Given these assumptions, let's see how we can structure our components.

Starting with the markup alone avoids cognitive overload. It might look like this:

```
<form class="editor">
  <textarea>User writes here</textarea>
  <div class="counter">Count goes here</div>
  <progress></progress>
</form>
```

To extract our presentational components, we can create a component for each visible UI element: we'll build one component for the <textarea>, one for the counter, and one for the progress. Let's call them Counter, ProgressBar, and Editor. The container parent component will calculate the word count and the progress and pass them as props to its children. Let's call it WordCounter. The final component structure will look like this:

```
<WordCounter>
  <Editor/>
  <Counter/>
  <ProgressBar/>
</WordCounter>
```

We've worked with container and presentational components and defined the component hierarchy for the word counter. Let's dive into designing individual components.

Design Presentational Components

Once we've decided on the general layout of the application, we can start working on the individual presentational components that make up the interface.

Styling with CSS is an important part of defining the appearance and functionality of a UI. CSS techniques such as BEM[4] strive to organize CSS classes into components, so that adding a component class to an element endows it with a bunch of properties. React makes these techniques less useful. With React, your whole interface is made up of React components. React components are much smaller than traditional templates, so each component encapsulates a potentially reusable part of the interface. By reusing React components, you automatically reuse the styles you define for each component, so CSS components are less useful. We'll use a CSS library called Tachyons,[5] which organizes individual CSS properties along regular increments to create a consistent appearance.

---

4. http://getbem.com
5. http://tachyons.io

Let's create a new directory for the word counter project. As before, we'll use a file named index.html in the top directory to provide the HTML skeleton. Create index.html and add the CDN link to Tachyons in index.html:

wordcounter-single/index.html
```
<!DOCTYPE html>
<html lang="en">
  <head>
    <meta charset="utf-8"/>
    <meta name="viewport" content="width=device-width, initial-scale=1"/>
    <link rel="stylesheet"
      href="https://unpkg.com/tachyons@4.8.0/css/tachyons.min.css"/>
  </head>
  <body>
    <div id="app"></div>
  </body>
</html>
```

From this point on, we'll store all our JavaScript sources in a directory named src. That way, we'll distinguish them more easily when we add additional configuration files to our project in the next chapters.

Create a new directory named src. Create a new file named index.js in the src directory and link it in index.html. Ensure there's a <div> with an id=*app*.

wordcounter-single/index.html
```
<body>
  <div id="app"></div>
  <script src="https://unpkg.com/react@15/dist/react.js"></script>
  <script src="https://unpkg.com/react-dom@15/dist/react-dom.js"></script>
  <script
          src="https://unpkg.com/babel-standalone@6/babel.min.js"
  ></script>
  <script type="text/babel" src="src/index.js"></script>
</body>
```

In index.js, define a function Counter() that outputs the value of its count prop in a <p> element:

wordcounter-single/src/index.js
```
function Counter({ count }) {
  return (
    <p className="mb2">
      Word count: {count}
    </p>
  );
}
```

Counter() expects an object with a count key. With destructuring, assign the value of the count parameter property to count in the Counter() body. Return a JSX expression with the count variable between braces to output a React element displaying its value. React uses className instead of class for legacy reasons and to avoid clashes with the JavaScript class keyword.

\// **Joe asks:**

ン゚ **Any more JSX gotchas?**

In addition to class and className, another difference between JSX and HTML is that you must use htmlFor instead of for to point a label to the element it labels. Probably the most important point to keep in mind when writing JSX is that React interprets elements that start with a capital letter as based on custom components, and elements that start with lowercase as plain HTML elements.

Next, create the progress bar component. In index.js, create a ProgressBar() function that takes a completion prop, and returns a progress bar with its value= attribute set to the completion prop:

```
wordcounter-single/src/index.js
function ProgressBar({ completion }) {
  const percentage = completion * 100;
  return (
    <div className="mv2 flex flex-column">
      <label htmlFor="progress" className="mv2">
        Progress
      </label>
      <progress value={completion} id="progress" className="bn">
        {percentage}%
      </progress>
    </div>
  );
}
```

<progress> is a standard HTML element. The value= attribute determines how much it fills. 0.5 means 50%, 0.6 means 60%, and so on, so completion should contain a number between 0 and 1. To make the progress bar accessible, we include a label for the <progress> element.

Next, let's create the text editor itself. In index.js, create an Editor component that defines a plain <textarea>. Editor takes the text as prop:

```
wordcounter-single/src/index.js
function Editor({
  text,
}) {
  return (
    <div className="flex flex-column mv2">
      <label htmlFor="editor" className="mv2">
        Enter your text:
      </label>
      <textarea
        value={text}
        id="editor"
      />
    </div>
  );
}
```

In HTML, the <textarea> child element determines the <textarea> content, but the <textarea> React element uses the value prop. Set the value prop of the <textarea> element to the value of the text prop.

You have almost all the ingredients in place. Now we'll combine Editor, ProgressBar, and Counter into a new component called WordCounter.

Assemble the Word Counter

While the other components map to a single user interface element, the WordCounter assembles the other components and computes their props. Since we can determine the word count and progress from the text and the target word count, it will take just two props: a text and a target word count. It will calculate the word count and progress and pass these values as props to Counter and ProgressBar.

We need to write some code to count the words in a string. When you've got code that has nothing to do with rendering a user interface, store it in a separate function. That way, you don't need to recreate the whole React element just to test the output of the function, and you can rearrange your components more easily as the functionality is not tied to a specific component. In index.js, define a new function named countWords() that counts the words in a string:

```
wordcounter-single/src/index.js
function countWords(text) {
  return text ? text.match(/\w+/g).length : 0;
}
```

The countWords() function accepts an argument with the text to count. We return 0 if text is null or undefined. Otherwise, we build an array of the words, separated by whitespace, and use its length as the word count. null and undefined behave as false in a boolean expression, and all other strings as true, so we use a ternary expression to distinguish the two cases. To count the words, use the match() function that's defined on all strings. match() takes a regular expression and returns an array containing the matching substring. To match a whitespace-separated word, use the /\w+/g regular expression. \w matches a non-space character, and the + sign means that every sequence of one or more characters counts as a single match. g indicates to return the substrings that match the pattern in the whole string. Call match() and pass it the regular expression, then retrieve the length property of the returned array.

Once you've defined the countWords() function, create the WordCounter() component. Define a new function named WordCounter() that takes an object with a text and targetWordCount properties. Pass text to countWords() to calculate the word count for Counter. From the word count, you can then calculate the progress for ProgressBar by dividing the word count by the target word count to obtain the progress.

wordcounter-single/src/index.js
```
function WordCounter({ text, targetWordCount }) {
  const wordCount = countWords(text);
  const progress = wordCount / targetWordCount;
}
```

Now that you've calculated the props for Counter and ProgressBar, we can display the complete interface. At the end of the WordCounter() function, combine Editor, Counter, and ProgressBar into a form, and pass the appropriate props to each element:

wordcounter-single/src/index.js
```
  const progress = wordCount / targetWordCount;
➤ return (
➤     <form className="measure pa4 sans-serif">
➤       <Editor text={text} />
➤       <div className="flex mt3">
➤         <Counter count={wordCount} />
➤         <ProgressBar completion={progress} />
➤       </div>
➤     </form>
➤ );
```

Place the child elements inside a <form> element. Pass text as the Editor text prop, wordCount as the Counter prop, and progress as the ProgressBar completion prop. Use braces instead of quotation marks after the equal sign; otherwise, React will interpret the props as string literals.

Let's render the word counter on the page. At the end of index.js, call ReactDOM.render() with the WordCounter component:

```
wordcounter-single/src/index.js
ReactDOM.render(
  <WordCounter text="Count the words in here." targetWordCount={10} />,
  document.getElementById('app')
);
```

Pass a string as the text prop and a number as the targetWordCount prop. Since the text prop is a string, you can enclose it in quotation marks. Render the word counter in the <div> with the *app* id=.

Include index.js in index.html after the React links and open index.html in the browser. You'll see the word counter displaying the text you set as the text prop and the matching count and progress. If you change the text and targetWordCount props and reload the page, the word count and the progress bar will update accordingly.

Most components should define the markup and style to display the data. They work a little bit like templates. Other components sit at the top of the component hierarchy, and calculate the data their children need.

What You Learned

In this chapter, you learned how to build React components, and you created a component that combines other components to make a word counter widget, using props to pass data between components. But there'a big piece missing: interactivity! In the next chapter, you'll learn about state and how to make React applications respond to user actions.

CHAPTER 2

Work with State and Events

Web applications are about dynamic data: you have to update the information you display in response to user actions and HTTP responses. In this chapter, you'll learn how to model data that changes over time, and you'll learn how to respond to user events and HTTP responses. You'll discover how to transform the word counter into a fully reactive interface.

Get to Know State

We'd like to allow users to edit the word counter text. For this, we need some way to handle values that change over time: a classic book asserts that an object has *state* if its behavior is influenced by its history (*Structure and Interpretation of Computer Programs [AS96]*).

Let's take a little detour to understand state. Open your browser's JavaScript console and type the add() function, which just adds its arguments together and returns the result:

```
uptospeed/src/functions.js
function add(x, y) {
  return x + y;
}
```

Then call the add() method a few times:

```
add(1,2); // returns 3
add(5, 7); // returns 12
add(1, 2); // returns 3 again
add(5, 7); // returns 12 again
```

The return value of add() depends only on its arguments, because it is a pure function.

Now type the addS() function, which multiplies the second argument by n before adding it to the first argument, and increments n each time you call it.

```
uptospeed/src/functions.js
let n = 1;

function addS(x, y) {
  const result = x + n * y;
  n++;
  return result;
}
```

The return value changes each time you call addS, even if the arguments stay the same, because the return value depends on how many times you've called addS. addS has a history: it stores state in the n variable.

The potential for bugs grows as the program grows. State complicates applications, as the same function, with the same arguments, can return different results based on when you call it.

We never tried to update a component's props inside the component itself, for a good reason: inside a React component, props are immutable (in practice, you can assign a new value to a prop inside a component, but it won't have any effect). To handle state, you need an additional mechanism. One good option is learning the tools that React itself provides. They get the job done in the majority of situations with little boilerplate.

Define the Application State

React defines a series of constraints that help you keep the application structure predictable. You must store the state that affects the UI in a dedicated object that you access with this.state. Once you set the initial value, you update this.state with the this.setState() function. setState() can only update the state of the component where you call it. To update other components, pass the state or values you compute based on the state as props. Since you can only pass props to child components, updates only flow from components down to their children. This constraint makes the consequences of a state update more predictable, as you only need to look at the child components.

Let's start with the structure of our state object. To prevent things from getting out of sync, we must avoid duplicate state. State is often surprisingly small if you don't let it spill over the whole application. To identify the minimal amount of state, ask these two questions:

1. Does this value change over time?

2. Does this value derive from other values that change over time?

In the word counter we built in the previous chapter, the text, the count, and the progress change over time, but both the word count and the progress are derived from the text, so the text is the only state we need. As React requires the state to be an object, we'll represent it like this:

```
{ text: 'What the user typed.' }
```

Now that we've determined what the state is, we need to find a suitable component to host it. Since we can only pass the state from a component to its children, pick a parent component of all components that require access to the state or to data that's derived from the state. We've divided our application into a few presentational components and the WordCounter component which calculates props for the other components and handles the application logic, so we'll store the state in the WordCounter component.

In React's current design, a component declared as a function cannot have state. To use state inside a component, you must declare that component using a JavaScript class. Let's turn WordCounter into a class. We'll continue working in the same directory as in the previous chapter. Open index.js and modify the WordCounter declaration:

```
wordcounter-single/src/index.js
class WordCounter extends React.Component {
}
```

To create a class component, define the class with the class keyword, followed by the class name. All React component classes must extend the React.Component class. React.Component defines setState(). By extending React.Component, a class can access setState() in turn. Use extends followed by the name of the class you want to extend.

In a class component, the render() function defines the UI. It returns a React.createElement() call or the equivalent JSX. Move the body of the WordCounter() function into a function named render() inside the WordCounter class:

```
wordcounter-single/src/index.js
render() {
  const { targetWordCount } = this.props;
  const { text } = this.state;
  const wordCount = countWords(text);
  const progress = wordCount / targetWordCount;

  return (
    <form className="measure pa4 sans-serif">
      <Editor
        text={text}
      />
```

```
    <Counter count={wordCount} />
    <ProgressBar completion={progress} />
  </form>
 );
}
```

To declare a function inside a class, use the function name followed by brackets, without the function keyword. Props and state don't get passed to the render() function. Instead, they're attached to the this variable. this is available in any function inside the class, so you can also access props and state outside the render() function if you need them. Retrieve the text value from this.state and the targetWordCount prop from this.props with a destructuring assignment. Destructuring allows you to rapidly retrieve the object property values by enclosing the property name with braces. JavaScript then assigns the object property value to the variable with the same name as the property, so target-WordCount has the same value as this.props.targetWordCount, and text has the same value as this.state.text.

We're done converting WordCounter to a class. this.state now determines the text. Currently, this.state.text starts as undefined, but we still need to render the word counter correctly before the user has typed something. We need to set a default value for this.state.text.

Since the box starts empty, we'll initialize this.state.text to an empty string. In the WordCounter class, create a function called constructor() to initialize the text:

wordcounter-single/src/index.js
```
constructor() {
  super();
  this.state = { text: '' };
}
```

The JavaScript runtime calls constructor() every time it creates a class instance. Inside constructor(), this points to the new instance. Add super() as the first line in constructor(). When a class extends another, JavaScript forces you to call super() before accessing this in the constructor. super() calls the superclass constructor() function to ensure that the superclass does the work it needs on the new object.

Since we're not using the text prop anymore, remove the text prop from the ReactDOM.render() call:

wordcounter-single/src/index.js
```
ReactDOM.render(
  <WordCounter targetWordCount={10} />,
  document.getElementById('app')
);
```

Reload the page to make sure everything works. Try changing the value for this.state in constructor() to check that the text area contents match the initial state. If the application doesn't work correctly, make sure you're retrieving text and targetWordCount from this.state and this.props, respectively.

We've converted WordCounter to a class and initialized its state. Let's connect the <textarea> to the word counter state so that typing updates the text.

Update the State with Events

We've set an initial value for the state. To update it, we need to capture user interactions such as typing or clicking.

In a React component, most user interactions generate an *event*. An event is an object that tells you which part of the interface has been affected (event.target) and what exactly happened (event.type). An *event handler* is a function that React calls every time it detects an event like a click or keyboard input. React passes the event as the first argument to the event handler, so you can use the event information to decide how to update the state. To make React call an event handler, you pass the event handler as a prop to the element where you want to capture the user interaction.

In our example, we want to update this.state in the word counter whenever the user changes the <textarea> content. To do so, we need to pass an event handler to the <textarea> element. But we also want to isolate the Editor implementation so that we can modify its internal element structure without affecting other components. We don't care about whether Editor uses <textarea> or a different element to build its user interface, as long as it lets us retrieve the text every time the user types. That's why we won't expose directly to other components the events generated in the <textarea>. Instead, we'll define two event handlers. We will pass one as a prop to the <Editor> element. Let's call this event handler handleTextChange(). We'll define handleTextChange() in WordCounter. That way, the event handler will be able to access this.setState(), and we will keep the logic together in the WordCounter component. Inside the Editor, we'll define a second event handler that we'll pass as a prop to the <textarea> element. This one will extract the current text from the event that <textarea> generates every time the user types and call handleTextChange() with the current text.

Open the file where you defined the WordCounter class. Add a new function, handleTextChange(), to WordCounter:

```
wordcounter-single/src/index.js
handleTextChange(currentText) {
  this.setState(() => ({ text: currentText }));
}
```

currentText represents the current contents of the input box. Call this.setState() to replace this.state.text with the new value.

setState() takes a function, which must return an object with the updated state properties. React merges the current state with this object, overwriting the values of any already defined properties with the new ones.

To define the argument to setState(), use the arrow function notation. First, write the function arguments. In this case, there are none, so just use empty parentheses. After the arrow, place the function return value. To replace the current value of this.state.text with the value of currentText, return an object with its text property set to currentText. JavaScript uses braces both to delimit the function body as well as to define objects. To remove the ambiguity, wrap the returned object in parentheses.

In the introduction to this chapter, you learned about pure functions. The function you pass to setState() must also be pure; it should just return a new object without modifying existing variables.

We've defined an event handler that updates WordCounter whenever it receives a new text. To let React call the event handler, you need to connect it to the <textarea>. Each user interaction corresponds to an event, like click, hover, and so on. Each event corresponds to a prop. For example, click has onClick, and hover has onHover. When you assign a function to that prop, React calls the function each time the event fires. Follow the same naming convention and create an onTextChange prop for the Editor component. First, pass handleTextChange() as a prop to the Editor component.

```
wordcounter-single/src/index.js
return (
  <form className="measure pa4 sans-serif">
    <Editor
      onTextChange={this.handleTextChange}
      text={text}
    />
    <Counter count={wordCount} />
    <ProgressBar completion={progress} />
  </form>
);
```

Next, modify the signature of the Editor() function to add the new onTextChange prop and create a new handleChange() function that passes the current <textarea> value to onTextChange():

```
wordcounter-single/src/index.js
function Editor({
  text,
```

```
➤     onTextChange
    }) {
      function handleChange(event) {
        onTextChange(event.target.value);
      }
      return (
        <div className="flex flex-column mv2">
          <label htmlFor="editor" className="mv2">
            Enter your text:
          </label>
          <textarea
            value={text}
➤           onChange={handleChange}
            id="editor"
          />
        </div>
      );
    }
```

Set the onChange= prop of the <textarea> element to the onChange() function. React will invoke onChange() every time the <textarea> contents change. It will pass onChange() an event object. Access the element that generated the event through the event target property. event.target points to the <textarea> element, and event.target.value to the <textarea> contents. onChange() calls onTextChange() with the <textarea> contents. In turn, onTextChange() calls this.setState() in WordCounter and replaces this.state.text with the <textarea> contents.

Now we have an issue. We must call the setState() method that WordCounter inherits from React.Component. In JavaScript, this changes meaning depending on context. Inside an event handler, this might not even be defined. To make sure this.setState() points to the setState() function in WordCounter at the time when React calls handleChange(), bind the function to this in the constructor:

wordcounter-single/src/index.js
```
constructor() {
  super();
  this.state = { text: '' };
➤ this.handleTextChange = this.handleTextChange.bind(this);
}
```

bind() returns a new function where this always has the value that it had when you called bind(). In the constructor, this points to the newly created wordCounter instance, so now this.setState() will be defined when React calls handleChange().

You can finally reload the page and type in some text. As you type, React invokes handleChange(), which in turn calls setState(). As the state changes, React schedules a re-render of the whole WordCounter component, which also triggers a re-render of its children. The result is that the count and progress bar appear to update in real time as you type.

This concludes our introduction to handling user-generated events. You've learned to define a class component, define event handlers, and update the state with setState(). Next, we'll look at another common source of state updates in web applications—talking to a web server.

Handle Asynchronous Events

You already know how to update the application state in response to user actions. Another common scenario is updating the state based on the response from a remote server. What makes this different is that communications like this are *asynchronous*, meaning the server request goes on in the background while your code keeps running. Nevertheless, setState() also fits the bill when you need to update the state in response to a server. As an example, we'll add save functionality to the word counter. This will show you how to use multiple states in the same application.

When the user clicks Save, the word counter sends the text they've typed to a server. When the server returns a successful response, we'll display a success message, and when it returns a failure response, we'll display a failure message. The final interface will look like this:

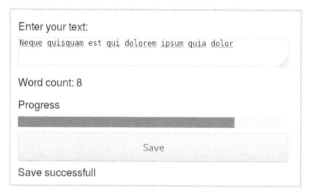

Our React application doesn't care whether the request really travels over HTTP, so instead of creating a real server, we'll set up a function that simulates a request and response. To make HTTP requests, browsers expose the fetch() function. fetch() takes a URL and returns a promise. A promise represents a result that might not be available immediately and defines a few functions that allow you to access the result when it's finally there.

Instead of calling fetch(), we'll create our own function called makeFakeRequest(). Our makeFakeRequest() function will return a promise. For more realism, we'll make the promise error out half the time. To simulate the time needed to send data across the network, we'll also wait a bit before returning a result.

In index.js, create a function called makeFakeRequest() that simulates a network request:

```
wordcounter-single/src/index.js
function makeFakeRequest() {
  return new Promise((resolve, reject) => {
  });
}
```

We call new Promise() to create a promise. The function you pass to the Promise() constructor determines whether the promise resolves with the expected result or an error and how long it takes to resolve:

```
wordcounter-single/src/index.js
function makeFakeRequest() {
  return new Promise((resolve, reject) => {
➤    setTimeout(() => {
➤      if (Math.random() > 0.5) {
➤        resolve('Success!');
➤      } else {
➤        reject('Failure');
➤      }
➤    }, 500);
  });
}
```

First, we introduce the delay. setTimeout() is a built-in JavaScript function that runs another function after a delay. setTimeout() takes the function to run and the delay expressed in milliseconds. Call setTimeout() and pass 500 as the second argument to delay execution by half a second.

After the delay has elapsed, we signal that the promise completed by using the resolve and reject arguments. resolve and reject are functions. We call resolve() to signal that the promise completed successfully and reject() to signal an error.

To introduce some randomness in the result, we call Math.random() to generate a random number between 0 and 1. If the number is greater than 0.5, we make the promise successful with resolve(). Otherwise, we mark the promise as failed with reject().

Now that you've got the function to simulate a network request, let's determine whether the save functionality requires some new state:

1. Do we have data that changes over time?

2. Can we derive this data from other data?

State can just be about how certain UI elements display. The save status certainly changes over time. We can't derive the save status from other data either, so we'll store in this.state.

Let's think about how to represent the save status. There are four different situations: either the save succeeded, it failed, it's in progress, or no save was attempted. We'll identify each situation with a constant. Create four constants inside index.js:

wordcounter-single/src/index.js

```
const SUCCESS = 'SUCCESS';
const FAILURE = 'FAILURE';
const WAITING = 'WAITING';
const IDLE = 'IDLE';
```

We'll then use the constants in this.state to indicate the situation we're in. For example, if the save is in progress, this.state will look like this:

```
{ saveStatus: WAITING }
```

Now that we've defined the state, let's design our components. Following our pattern of separating state management from display of information, our save button and information label will be presentational components that just show the props they get. We'll call these two components SaveButton and AlertBox.

We must decide in which component to store the save state. Should we store it in the top WordCounter component? There are trade-offs involved here. Pushing all state in the top component gives you a single point of control, but passing props through too many components can make it difficult to track where the data is coming from and degrades performance. In Chapter 5, *Using Redux as a Central Data Store*, on page 63, we'll learn about a pattern to keep all our state in a central store. For this example, we'll create a new component dedicated to managing the save process, called SaveManager.

Let's create the presentational components. First, create the SaveButton component:

wordcounter-single/src/index.js

```
function SaveButton({ onClick }) {
  return (
    <button className="pv2 ph3" onClick={onClick}>
      Save
    </button>
  );
}
```

The save button takes a single prop, onClick(), which is a function to call when the user clicks the button. It returns a <button> element that triggers onClick() when clicked. Since this button is decoupled from the application, we could share it across many projects, or replace it with a pre-made component from one of the many third-party libraries.

Then, create the AlertBox component:

```
wordcounter-single/src/index.js
function AlertBox({ status }) {
  if (status === FAILURE) {
    return <div className="mv2">Save failed</div>;
  } else if (status === SUCCESS) {
    return <div className="mv2">Save successful</div>;
  } else if (status === WAITING) {
    return <div className="mv2">Saving…</div>;
  } else {
    return null;
  }
}
```

AlertBox takes a string prop, status. Compare the value of status with the constants you defined before. If status equals FAILURE, display the failure message; if status equals SUCCESS, display the success message; and if status equals WAITING, display the waiting message. When status equals IDLE, we don't want to display any message. When you return null from a component, React doesn't render anything.

With the two presentational components out of the way, let's tackle the Save-Manager component. Create a new class component that extends React.Component:

```
wordcounter-single/src/index.js
class SaveManager extends React.Component {
}
```

Our component needs the text to save, so we pass it as a prop from the word counter. Since we pass the data, we also pass the function to save it. The two change together. If the data changes shape, the function to save it does too.

In the SaveManager class, create a function named save() to invoke when the user clicks the save button:

```
wordcounter-single/src/index.js
save(event) {
  event.preventDefault();
  this.setState(() => ({ saveStatus: WAITING }));
  this.props
    .saveFunction(this.props.data)
    .then(
      success => this.setState(() => ({ saveStatus: SUCCESS })),
      failure => this.setState(() => ({ saveStatus: FAILURE }))
    );
}
```

We call event.preventDefault() to stop the form from submitting, and then call save-Function() on the data to save. Since saveFunction() returns a promise, we must wait to access the result. Promises define a then() function, which takes two other functions as arguments. Once the promise completes, the functions that you pass to then() retrieve the result and handle errors. We handle a successful result in the first function. In this case, we set state.saveStatus to SUCCESS. We handle errors in the second function. In that case, we set the state to FAILURE.

Now let's connect the save() function and the save status to the UI. Create the SaveManager render() function and pass saveStatus and save() to AlertBox and SaveButton:

wordcounter-single/src/index.js
```
render() {
  return (
    <div className="flex flex-column mv2">
      <SaveButton onClick={this.save} />
      <AlertBox status={this.state.saveStatus} />
    </div>
  );
}
```

Since we pass the state to the alert box, every time we call setState() in SaveManager, the alert box also re-renders with the updated state. There are still two things left to do.

Inside the save button component, the this keyword in the event handler attached with onClick refers to the <button> element. To remedy this, define a constructor() function in SaveManager to create a new function where this always points to the SaveManager component:

wordcounter-single/src/index.js
```
constructor() {
  super();
  this.save = this.save.bind(this);
}
```

First, call super() to invoke React.Component's constructor. Then call bind() on this.save and reassign the result to this.save.

The second issue is that we want to make the status indicator start in the correct state when the application first loads. Initialize this.state.saveStatus to IDLE:

wordcounter-single/src/index.js
```
constructor() {
  super();
  this.save = this.save.bind(this);
  this.state = { saveStatus: IDLE };
}
```

With these changes, the save functionality is ready. In the WordCounter render() function, insert the SaveManager element before the closing <form> tag:

wordcounter-single/src/index.js
```
  <Counter count={wordCount} />
  <ProgressBar completion={progress} />
➤ <SaveManager saveFunction={makeFakeRequest} data={this.state} />
</form>
```

Reload the page and click Save. The alert box appears, showing the Saving… message, then switching to either success or failure. You might need to click a few times to see both messages at least once. When you click the button, you invoke the callback, which sets state to loading and starts the request. When the request completes, it sets the state to either success or error.

Even though a network response and a user action might look different, you can handle both in a similar way with React's setState().

What You Learned

React encourages you to pay attention to data that evolves over time: the state of your application. For most applications, you handle this data with the setState() function. Event handlers let you know how users interact with the UI and update the state in response. You've also learned to update the state in response to some new data from the network.

You've got a sizable amount of code and many components, but it all works, and it's time to put the component into production. Your giant file is becoming unwieldy. In the next chapter, you'll see how to split the code into modules without sacrificing performance.

CHAPTER 3

Create a Production Build

Many applications that rely on sophisticated JavaScript components fail to live up to their potential because they load slowly. Here, you'll learn how to spare your own creations from this fate.

Let's look at the word counter we've built in the previous two chapters. We need four network requests: one to download React, one to download React-DOM, one to download Babel, and one for the word counter itself. Loading speed is critical for user satisfaction,[1] but people can't start using the app until the last file downloads.

As an application grows, it's tempting to split the code across multiple files so we can navigate the project more easily as we modify things. For example, we might place the SaveManager component in its own file. But if we did that, we would increase the loading time even more; if we had a separate file for every component, we would need to download even more separate files, and we'd also struggle to remember how to include them in the right order in the HTMl page.

We'll solve this dilemma with a module bundler called webpack.[2] Modules let you divide an application into multiple files, each with a specific function, and define the dependencies between the files. Then the module bundler aggregates the source files into as many or as little files as you want. It automatically assembles the modules in the right order, so you end up with a single file to serve.

webpack can also transform the source code before assembling the modules, so use Babel to turn JSX into React.createElement() calls in advance. In this way, we'll get rid of the in-browser Babel transform that's too slow for production.

---

1. https://wpostats.com/
2. https://webpack.js.org

This means you can optimize for performance in production while keeping the source files in a structure that's optimal for ease of development. Let's get started.

Set Up the Development Environment

To use webpack and Babel, you must install Node.js on your computer. Refer to the instructions on the Node.js website[3] to install Node.js for your operating system. Both the long-term-support (LTS) and the latest release should work, but generally, the LTS version is a safer choice. If you already have Node.js installed, ensure it's at least the latest release in the 6.x series. The application won't need Node.js installed to run; you'll only need Node.js to prepare the files before you upload them to your web server.

Once you have installed Node.js, check that the npm command is on your PATH. The Node.js installer should set things up correctly, but double-check by running npm --version in your terminal:

```
$ npm --version
5.3.0
```

If the npm version is less than 3, some of the examples in this book might not work and you might need to use a more recent Node.js version.

JavaScript build tools and practices are in flux, so it makes sense to isolate the build tools and dependencies for each project; this way, incompatible versions won't clash with each other. npm is the Node.js package manager, but it also offers a lot of functionality to run builds in a repeatable and cross-platform way. We'll use the npm command to manage our build and isolate each project's dependencies.

Navigate into the directory where you created the word counter. We're going to turn it into an npm package by adding a package.json. package.json documents your project dependencies and allows anyone to reinstall a compatible version that only your project can access. The npm init command creates a starting package.json automatically. Type:

```
$ npm init -y
```

The -y switch chooses a set of default configuration options for your project. Most of these options only matter if you plan to publish your project, so you can accept the defaults.

---

3.   https://nodejs.org

The directory structure for the project now looks like this:

```
└── wordcounter/
        ├── package.json
        ├── index.html
        ├── src/
```

The package.json file stores the project information. By the time we'll complete this chapter and the next, it will look something like this:

```
wordcounter/package.json
{
  "name": "wordcounter",
  "version": "1.0.0",
  "description": "",
  "private": true,
  "main": "index.js",
  "scripts": {
    "test": "jest --watch",
    "library:build":
"cross-env NODE_ENV=production webpack -p --config webpack.config.library.js",
    "start": "cross-env NODE_ENV=development webpack-dev-server -d",
    "build": "cross-env NODE_ENV=production  webpack -p"
  },
  "author": "Ludovico Fischer",
  "license": "ISC",
  "devDependencies": {
    "babel-loader": "^7.1.0",
    "babel-preset-react-app": "^3.0.2",
    "cross-env": "^5.0.5",
    "jest": "^20.0.0",
    "react-test-renderer": "^15.6.0",
    "webpack-dev-server": "^2.6.1",
    "enzyme": "^2.9.0",
    "webpack": "^3.3.0"
  },
  "dependencies": {
    "react": "^15.6.1",
    "react-dom": "^15.6.1"
  }
}
```

We're mostly interested in the scripts, dependencies, and devDependencies sections. Other properties like name, description, and main are only useful if you want to publish your project, so you can ignore them. The scripts section defines commands to manage our project. package.json records development and production dependencies separately. Development dependencies are tools like webpack that you use to develop your code but won't need when it runs. Production dependencies are the libraries that you must distribute together with your code to make it run on users' browsers. Production dependencies go into the dependencies section, while development dependencies go into devDependencies section. Specifying this information allows someone else to install the required dependencies when they install your code with npm, but it's also very useful as documentation.

Now that we've transformed our project into an npm package, install the webpack[4] module bundler and record it as a development dependency with this command:

```
$ npm i --save-dev webpack
```

i stands for install. --save-dev saves the version of webpack in package.json as a development dependency. If you leave the repository URL empty, npm will issue warnings every time you run a command. You can ignore them or add "private": "true" to package.json to silence them.

Open package.json to see the new devDependencies section that npm created.

wordcounter/package.json
```
"devDependencies": {
  "webpack": "^3.3.0"
},
```

To indicate acceptable versions of a library or tool, npm uses special characters in front of the version numbers. npm packages are encouraged to follow semantic versioning[5] to express compatibility between versions. If a package breaks compatibility with a previous version, the author should change the first number; the caret ^ means that the package is compatible with all webpack versions that start with 3.

npm stores the libraries you install and their dependencies in the node_modules directory inside the current directory. Delete node_modules, and re-install all your dependencies with:

```
$ npm install
```

npm reads the project dependencies from package.json and installs the webpack version required to build the project.

If you're using npm 5.0.0 or greater, you might have noticed that npm printed this message when you installed webpack:

```
npm notice created a lockfile as package-lock.json. You should commit this file.
```

---

4.   https://webpack.github.io
5.   http://semver.org

package-lock.json records the exact version of every package and of its dependencies to provide even more reproducible builds.

You now have npm running and you can install the packages you need to create your application. Next, let's start setting up the build.

Configure webpack

Now that you've installed webpack, let's create the webpack configuration file so we can bundle our project. Depending on your application, it might make sense to split its code across multiple files or aggregate everything into a single file. webpack assembles the source files in a different set of files for deployment. This way you can always choose the most efficient deployment strategy, without changing your source code layout. In an application with multiple screens, you could place all dependencies that are used in every screen in one file, and the code for each screen in a separate file. That way the user only downloads the code for the page they visit. For simple applications like our word counter, which only has a single page, it's sufficient to put everything into a single file. This will speed up the time it takes to download the app by reducing network requests.

A minimal webpack configuration requires one or more entry points and one output. Entry points configure the files where execution starts once the application loads in the browser. The output configures how entry points map to output file names. We will also ask webpack to transform our original source code, replacing JSX code with calls to React.createElement().

Let's start with the entry points. Place the webpack configuration in a file named webpack.config.js in the project directory:

```
├── webpack.config.js
└── src/
    ├── index.js
```

The webpack configuration is a JavaScript object that you assign to a variable called module.exports in webpack.config.js.

wordcounter/webpack.config.js
```
module.exports = {
};
```

Although we'll produce just one output file, we'll name each entry point. That way it will be easier to add more entry points when you create more advanced webpack configurations. Open webpack.config.js and add index.js as an entry point:

```
wordcounter/webpack.config.js
module.exports = {
  entry: { app: './src/index.js' },
};
```

The value of the entry key is an object where each key represents an entry point name, and the value represents the path to the file relative to web-pack.config.js. Name the index.js entry point app, and be sure to include the leading dot in the file path; otherwise, webpack will complain that it cannot find the file.

Now that you've configured the entry point, let's configure the output files. That's where webpack places the result of aggregating the modules. We'll add a new property called output, which points to the absolute filesystem path of the output bundle. To ensure that absolute path definitions work whether you're using Windows or a Unix-based operating system, you'll define the output path with a Node.js function. Add this line at the top of webpack.config.js:

```
wordcounter/webpack.config.js
const path = require('path');
```

This imports a Node.js module to manipulate filesystem paths. There's some work in progress to support the same JavaScript module system everywhere. The Node.js module system predates the one we'll use in our application, so try not to get too confused by this.

Then tell webpack to output the bundled modules in an app-bundle.js file in the current directory.

```
wordcounter/webpack.config.js
output: {
  path: path.resolve(__dirname),
  filename: '[name]-bundle.js'
},
```

Specify the output directory with the path property. The variable __dirname (with two underscores at the start) points to the current directory, and path.resolve() uses the path module you just imported to output the absolute path from the filesystem root to the current directory. Then name the output file with the filename property. Include the entry name in the output name so you'll be able to distinguish the source of different output files. webpack replaces [name] with the entry point name—in this case, app—so the output file name will be app-bundle.js.

After we have specified the entry and the output, we will tell webpack to transform our source with Babel. webpack's module concept extends beyond JavaScript files; webpack considers any file that it knows how to concatenate with others and output into a bundle as a module. You can extend this with webpack add-ons called *loaders*, which are functions that transform or analyze the source code before webpack places it in the final output. Loaders process JavaScript, as well as CSS and even fonts and images, so any file type in your web application can become a module.

To tell webpack how to transform the source code, we need to add a loader and some rules that tell webpack which files we want to transform. We'll do this in a new object inside the webpack configuration file. Create an object named module, then add an array called rules inside the module object. Each entry in the rules array contains rules to select a subset of the project files and the name of the loader that processes those files. To use Babel to transform the files with the .js extension in the src directory, add an entry with the "babel-loader" string:

```
wordcounter/webpack.config.js
module.exports = {
  entry: { app: './src/index.js' },
  output: {
    path: path.resolve(__dirname),
    filename: '[name]-bundle.js'
  },
➤  module: {
➤    rules: [
➤      {
➤        test: /\.js$/,
➤        include: path.resolve(__dirname, 'src'),
➤        use: ['babel-loader']
➤      }
➤    ]
➤  }
➤};
```

Each element in the rules array defines a type of file and the loaders to use for those files. webpack recognizes file types from their file names and locations on the file system. We select the target file names with the test regular expression—in this case, all files with a .js extension. The dependencies in node_modules should already have been bundled correctly by their maintainers, so we skip them to speed up the build. To process only the src directory, add an include property with the path to the src directory. The use array contains the list of loaders to use—in this case, just babel-loader. That takes care of the webpack configuration. Next, we'll configure the Babel transformation.

> \\//   **Joe asks:**
> `<`   **This feels like a chore. Can't we take a shortcut?**
>
> Once you understand what's involved in the build, you can skip most of these steps
> by using react-create-app.[a] This npm package lets you set up a build for a React
> application with a single command. But to use different libraries like CSS preprocessors
> or certain UI toolkits, you'll still need to dig into webpack, so it's important that you
> get a good picture of how it works.
>
> _____
>
> a.   https://github.com/facebookincubator/create-react-app

Configure Babel

Outside of a browser, Babel only runs the transformations you explicitly
indicate, so we need to supply a list of transformations for Babel to do anything. To speed up the configuration process, we'll use the react-app preset,
which combines the most useful options for React applications. This preset
includes JSX support, as well as other options that support most common
browsers and the testing environment we'll use in Chapter 4, *Test Your React
Components*, on page 49. Install Babel, the Babel loader, and the react-app
preset from npm:

```
$ npm i --save-dev babel-loader babel-core babel-preset-react-app
```

You'll need to install the Babel core dependency explicitly because the Babel
loader developers decided to let you choose which Babel version to use. We'll
just go with the default.

To apply the react-app preset, create a Babel configuration file called .babelrc in
the root of the project directory. In .babelrc, add the react-app preset to the presets
array to tell Babel to process the source code with the preset:

```
wordcounter/.babelrc
{
  "presets": ["react-app"]
}
```

We're done with the webpack and Babel configuration. Now let's create a
script that runs the build for us.

Run Your Build

If we run the webpack command directly, we need to set up the path to the webpack executable and look up the right command-line options every time we run

the build. Instead, we will create an entry in the scripts section of package.json that describes the build command, so we'll be able to build the project with the correct options by typing only npm build.

Before we create the build command, we need to install a utility called cross-env to set environment variables in a way that works both for Windows and Unix systems:

```
$ npm i --save-dev cross-env
```

Once you've downloaded cross-env, open package.json, and in the scripts section, create a new entry to run the build. When it installs an executable, npm places the executable in the node_modules/.bin directory and automatically looks in that location if you don't specify a path in a script. One annoyance is that we need to define our environment twice—once for Babel and once for webpack. The react-app preset applies different transformations depending on the value of the NODE_ENV environment variables. Use cross-env to set the NODE_ENV to 'production'. This makes sure that Babel applies all the production optimizations. The -p activates production mode for webpack, which turns on minification and replaces occurrences of the process.env in the code that webpack builds.

```
wordcounter/package.json
"scripts": {
  "build": "cross-env NODE_ENV=production  webpack -p"
},
```

Minification shortens variable and function names throughout the source, often to single letters. On top of reducing download times, minification also reduces the time the JavaScript engine needs to parse the code. These techniques often yield very large decreases in file size; you might not feel much difference from a high-speed wired connection in an urban area, but as soon as you navigate on a crowded Wi-Fi network on a train, or if you attempt to connect from a rural area, the loading times will differ hugely.

The -p switch also replaces the process.env variable with the 'production' string whenever process.env appears in the source code. Right now, this doesn't change anything, as we're not using process.env in our own code, but it will turn useful when we install React from npm.

Let's test our build command. Type npm run build in the project's directory to launch the build.

webpack prints the files it creates along with their sizes. The app-bundle.js file contains the resulting application code.

```
$ npm run build
cross-env NODE_ENV=production  webpack -p

Hash: 8ce725308ddb93d694b7
Version: webpack 3.5.4
Time: 3718ms
        Asset    Size  Chunks              Chunk Names
app-bundle.js  151 kB       0  [emitted]  app
  [77] ./src/saveStatus.js 121 bytes {0} [built]
  [78] ./src/index.js 346 bytes {0} [built]
 [171] ./src/WordCounter.js 3.94 kB {0} [built]
 [172] ./src/ProgressBar.js 586 bytes {0} [built]
 [173] ./src/Counter.js 489 bytes {0} [built]
 [174] ./src/Editor.js 516 bytes {0} [built]
 [175] ./src/SaveManager.js 3.38 kB {0} [built]
 [176] ./src/SaveButton.js 224 bytes {0} [built]
 [177] ./src/AlertBox.js 603 bytes {0} [built]
 [178] ./src/countWords.js 104 bytes {0} [built]
 [179] ./src/makeFakeRequest.js 377 bytes {0} [built]
     + 169 hidden modules
```

To test the minimized code, open index.html and replace index.js with app-bundle.js. Since you don't need the in-browser Babel transform any more, remove the babel.min.js script from index.html and remove the *text/babel* type= attribute.

wordcounter/index.html
```
<script src="app-bundle.js"></script>
```

Reload the page to check that the application renders as before. If you get a blank page instead, check the webpack output to see if it encountered an error while processing the files.

You've configured both webpack and Babel to create an optimized production build, but during development, it's more convenient to have a faster build and to preserve more verbose error messages, so next we'll look at a variation on our build commands that offers a better development experience.

Speed Up Feedback

While the production build performs the best, it's more comfortable to use a different build environment for development. Creating the production build is slow, and the -p switch and minification lose many helpful warnings and error messages.

To improve the development experience, we'll create a separate build script for development and replace webpack with webpack-dev-server. webpack-dev-server is a web server that builds and serves the application bundle from memory, so that the build process takes less time. We'll set up a second npm script with different environment variables to use the React development build, and we'll keep our existing build script unchanged.

Install webpack-dev-server with npm:

```
$ npm i --save-dev webpack-dev-server
```

Then create a new script to run webpack-dev-server. Set the NODE_ENV variable to development and activate source maps. Source maps are special files that map the location in the aggregated file to the original source, and allow the browser to point to the original file and line number when an error occurs. For source maps to work, you need to load the page from a web server: that's one more reason to use webpack-dev-server for development. The -d switch activates source maps. Open package.json and add a new property named start to the scripts section:

wordcounter/package.json
```
"start": "cross-env NODE_ENV=development webpack-dev-server -d",
```

Once you've set up the start script, type

```
$ npm start
```

Then visit http://localhost:8080 to access your application. To see the page reload automatically, open index.js in your editor and change the word count legend. If there's trouble, check both the terminal console and the web browser console for error messages.

This setup allows you to iterate faster, keeping all the development warnings on and without waiting too long for the build to finish. Since webpack-dev-server serves file from memory, it doesn't update app-bundle.js on disk, so you must run npm run build to update app-bundle.js when you wish to make a release.

That's it for the build configuration. Now, we'll turn to the application code to see how we can best make use of modules.

Organize Your Code with Modules

Some web applications consist of a single JavaScript application that manages the whole page. In that case, it can make sense to include React in the application bundle. That way the browser does not make separate requests for React and ReactDOM. And since no other code uses React, there isn't the problem of downloading React twice. It's also a bit simpler to deploy since everything is included in one file, and you don't need to update the HTML source to include the correct React version. Finally, importing React as a module is the most flexible method: in Chapter 6, *Work Well with Others*, on page 85, we'll see that we can use an external React even if we import it as a module! So, to get started with modules, let's download the React module from npm and include React in our application that way.

Since webpack automatically finds modules you install from npm, the best way is to install React and ReactDOM from npm, then import them into your application as JavaScript modules. To get started, install React and ReactDOM:

```
$ npm i --save react react-dom
```

--save puts React and React DOM in the project dependencies, instead of its development dependencies like --save-dev. Development dependencies are only required to build the project, but dependencies are required to run the code in production.

We're now ready to import React and ReactDOM into your index.js file. To import a module you installed with npm, you just specify the npm package name. Add these lines at the top of index.js to import React and ReactDOM:

wordcounter/src/index.js
```
import React from 'react';
import ReactDOM from 'react-dom';
```

Save the file and run the build script again:

```
$ npm run build
```

This updates app-bundle.js. webpack reads the imports from each file and concatenates everything in the right order in app-bundle.js.

You can now remove React and ReactDOM from index.html, as the bundle includes them both. You'll be left with a single <script> tag in the document.

wordcounter/index.html
```
<script src="app-bundle.js"></script>
```

Reload the page to check that everything works.

In Chapter 1, *An Introduction to Components*, on page 1, you learned that React has a development build and a production build. The development build contains debugging code that makes React run slower, but provides better error messages and debugging information. The production build runs faster. The React package you download from npm uses the process.env variable to determine whether to include extra debugging code. The webpack configuration determines which React build ends up in your bundle. Use the -p switch to get the production build. If you omit -p, you'll get the development build, unless you create some webpack configuration by hand to replace the process.env variable with the 'production' string. You can use the full debugging configuration while you develop and switch to the optimized configuration to output the production build.

You can organize your own source code into separate modules, making them easier to navigate and maintain.

By default, a module cannot access anything that you define in a different module. You must mark the variables to expose to other files with the export keyword. In this way, you get explicit interfaces between the parts of the application, but there are no restrictions on a module's content, so you need to find a convention. The most obvious is to use one React component per module and name the files based on the component. To simplify tests, store code that's unrelated to React, like the countWords() function, in separate modules.

Our first step will be to separate the call to ReactDOM.render() from the component definitions. Open index.js and cut all code except the ReactDOM.render() call, then paste everything else in a new file named WordCounter.js in the src directory:

```
└── src/
    ├── index.js
    ├── WordCounter.js
```

Since you placed all of the WordCounter code in a separate file, you must import React again in that file. Babel translates JSX into React.createElement() calls, so import React whenever you use JSX to ensure React.createElement() is defined. In index.js, leave just the React import and the code that renders the WordCounter component:

wordcounter/src/index.js
```
import React from 'react';
import ReactDOM from 'react-dom';
ReactDOM.render(
  <WordCounter targetWordCount={20} />,
  document.getElementById('app')
);
```

Place the rest of the application code in WordCounter.js and import React at the top:

wordcounter/src/WordCounter.js
```
import React from 'react';
```

Now define the module interfaces. When you define a module, you must indicate which values will be available to other modules. This way, as you change the code inside one module, you will not introduce new variables into other modules by mistake. For the WordCounter module, we want just the WordCounter itself to be available to the main index.js file. We'll use a *default export* to achieve this.

A default export lets other files import WordCounter with the same syntax you used to import React. Place this line at the bottom of WordCounter.js:

wordcounter/src/WordCounter.js
```
export default WordCounter;
```

To indicate that WordCounter inside index.js refers to the WordCounter you've defined in a separate module, import WordCounter in index.js:

wordcounter/src/index.js
```
import React from 'react';
import ReactDOM from 'react-dom';
import WordCounter from './WordCounter';
ReactDOM.render(
  <WordCounter targetWordCount={20} />,
  document.getElementById('app')
);
```

You can reference npm modules like React with their name only. For modules in your own code, you must specify the relative path from the current file to the file containing the module you want to import. import makes the default export of the module after the from accessible in the current file. You can leave out the .js extension, as webpack resolves it automatically. With a default export, you can also name the import any way you want.

webpack traces module dependencies and aggregates related modules into a single file. In this way, you can use multiple files in development, without worrying about the loading order and excessive HTTP requests. webpack works with JavaScript modules out of the box, so test the build by running:

```
$ npm run build
```

If you get any errors, verify that you specified the path to the WordCounter module with a slash, because it's part of your own code base. Modules installed with npm are available just via their module names, so there's no slashes when you import React and ReactDOM.

Now that you've confirmed that webpack understands modules, let's split each component into a separate module. First, move the ProgressBar component into its own file. Create a new file called ProgressBar.js in the src directory. To use JSX, import React at the top of the file. At the end of the file, export the ProgressBar component:

wordcounter/src/ProgressBar.js
```
import React from 'react';

function ProgressBar({ completion }) {
  const percentage = completion * 100;
  return (
```

```
      <div className="mv2 flex flex-column">
        <label htmlFor="progress" className="mv2">
          Progress
        </label>
        <progress value={completion} id="progress" className="bn">
          {percentage}%
        </progress>
      </div>
    );
  }
```

➤ `export default ProgressBar;`

Do the same with Counter, Editor, and SaveManager. Next, create a module for the countWords() function. Cut the function definition and paste it into its own file, then export the function:

wordcounter/src/countWords.js
```
function countWords(text) {
  return text ? text.match(/\w+/g).length : 0;
}
```

`export default countWords;`

There's no need to import React here, since the function does not use any JSX.

Repeat these steps to extract the makeFakeRequest() function into a separate module in the makeFakeRequest.js file:

wordcounter/src/makeFakeRequest.js
```
function makeFakeRequest() {
  return new Promise((resolve, reject) => {
    setTimeout(() => {
      if (Math.random() > 0.5) {
        resolve('Success!');
      } else {
        reject('Failure');
      }
    }, 500);
  });
}
```

`export default makeFakeRequest;`

Since you removed ProgressBar, Counter, Editor, countWords(), and makeFakeRequest() from WordCounter.js, add an import statement on top of WordCounter.js to import them:

wordcounter/src/WordCounter.js
```
import React from 'react';
import ProgressBar from './ProgressBar';
import Counter from './Counter';
import Editor from './Editor';
import SaveManager from './SaveManager';
```

```
➤ import countWords from './countWords';
➤ import makeFakeRequest from './makeFakeRequest';
```

We're left with the SaveManager component. Let's create separate modules for SaveManager, SaveButton, and AlertBox. Cut each component from WordCounter and paste it in a new file in the src directory, named SaveManager.js, SaveButton.js, and AlertBox.js, respectively.

In SaveButton.js, import React and export the SaveButton component:

wordcounter/src/SaveButton.js
```
import React from 'react';

function SaveButton({ onClick }) {
  return (
    <button className="pv2 ph3" onClick={onClick}>
      Save
    </button>
  );
}

export default SaveButton;
```

AlertBox shares some constants with SaveManager. To use the constants in both files, extract the constants in a separate file named saveStatus.js and export each constant separately by using export without default:

wordcounter/src/saveStatus.js
```
export const SUCCESS = 'SUCCESS';
export const FAILURE = 'FAILURE';
export const WAITING = 'WAITING';
export const IDLE = 'IDLE';
```

The advantage of non-default exports is that you can put many in a single file. If we had used default exports, we would have had to create a separate file for each constant.

Once you've got the constants in a separate module, import React and the constants in AlertBox.js and export AlertBox:

wordcounter/src/AlertBox.js
```
import React from 'react';
import { SUCCESS, FAILURE, WAITING } from './saveStatus';

function AlertBox({ status }) {
  if (status === FAILURE) {
    return <div className="mv2">Save failed</div>;
  } else if (status === SUCCESS) {
    return <div className="mv2">Save successful</div>;
  } else if (status === WAITING) {
    return <div className="mv2">Saving…</div>;
  } else {
```

```
      return null;
    }
  }
}
```

export default AlertBox;

If you omit the default keyword in your export, then you must use the same name in the import as in the export, and place braces around the name.

Finally, import React, SaveButton, AlertBox, and the constants in SaveManager.js:

wordcounter/src/SaveManager.js

```
➤ import React from 'react';
➤ import SaveButton from './SaveButton';
➤ import AlertBox from './AlertBox';
➤ import { IDLE, SUCCESS, FAILURE, WAITING } from './saveStatus';

class SaveManager extends React.Component {
```

Then export SaveManager at the end of SaveManager.js:

wordcounter/src/SaveManager.js

export default SaveManager;

Usually, you'll place components in separate modules from the start, so you wouldn't have to do this work to split them up. The final layout should look like this:

```
└── src/
    ├── AlertBox.js
    ├── Counter.js
    ├── countWords.js
    ├── Editor.js
    ├── index.js
    ├── makeFakeRequest.js
    ├── ProgressBar.js
    ├── saveStatus.js
    ├── SaveButton.js
    ├── SaveManager.js
    ├── WordCounter.js
```

With the components organized in modules, you can get an overview of the app by looking at the files on disk. You also know that each file contains one React component with the same name, so you know where to find any component you come across in the code.

To make sure everything still works, start the application again:

```
$ npm start
```

Open index.html and interact with the application. Watch out for any error output in the terminal, as well errors in the browser console. A common problem is forgetting to export anything from a module, in which case the import will be undefined.

What You Learned

You've improved loading times for your application by creating an optimized build and converting JSX before deploying, and you relied on npm to isolate your project dependencies. You configured a faster build for development, which preserves the debug information. The build step allowed you to organize your code with modules without slowing down your application excessively.

In a larger code base, it's important that you can test your components so that you don't need to verify the entire application by hand every time you make a change. In the next chapter, we'll extend the setup we created to add tests to our project and learn testing techniques for React components.

CHAPTER 4

Test Your React Components

Manually navigating through a large application to check that everything works is too time consuming. It's better to test parts of the application with automated tests.

When the UI makes a substantial part of the application, it's difficult to create automated tests that not only inform you of errors but also require reasonably little code.

One option would be to use a browser automation library to navigate through your application, but this sort of test tends to fail in ways that are difficult to interpret. It also takes a long time to set up, so it's only useful for testing at a high level. It also doesn't require any React-specific knowledge, so I encourage you to refer to other books or resources to learn more about it. If you're interested in end-to-end testing in JavaScript, take a look at Nightwatch.js.[1] *The Way of the Web Tester*, also published by the Pragmatic Bookshelf, is a good guide to all the different ways to test a web application.

Instead of browser automation, we'll test React applications without starting a browser. You'll set up a test framework for the word counter and then test the plain functions that contain the application logic. You'll then test the render output of a single component and verify the interaction of a parent component with its children. Each of these techniques tests an isolated slice of your application, making the tests faster to write and to run. And they'll be more informative when they fail.

---

1.   http://nightwatchjs.org/

Set Up the Test Framework

Let's add some tests to the word counter project. We'll start by installing a test framework that runs our tests and reports the test results. We'll use Jest[2] because it offers an excellent out-of-the-box experience, but you can apply the techniques you'll learn to other test frameworks.

Navigate to the word counter project directory and install Jest as a development dependency:

```
$ npm i --save-dev jest
```

Since your code uses JSX, you also need to transpile the code when you run the tests. A Jest plugin called babel-jest ensures Jest transpiles the test code with the Babel configuration it finds in the package root. Install the babel-jest plugin as a development dependency:

```
$ npm i --save-dev babel-jest
```

We'll use npm scripts to run our tests via the npm command. That way, you'll avoid conflicts between different versions of Jest in different projects.

The jest utility scans the directory for files with names that end in test or spec, or files in a directory named _tests_. It then executes the tests they contain. Since there's no single dominant testing tool for JavaScript, the npm test command is the standard way to run tests in projects managed with npm. Open package.json and modify the test entry in the scripts section in package.json to run the local version of Jest with the npm test command:

```
wordcounter/package.json
"scripts": {
  "test": "jest --watch",
```

The --watch flag lets Jest automatically re-run the tests when you edit a file. To check that your setup works, run:

```
$ npm test
```

Jest reports the regular expression used to find test files. It automatically ignores node_modules. Since you haven't written any tests yet, Jest hasn't run any tests.

```
No tests found
14 files checked.
roots: wordcounter - 14 matches
testMatch: **/__tests__/**/*.js?(x),**/?(*.)(spec|test).js?(x) - 0 matches
testPathIgnorePatterns: /node_modules/ - 14 matches
```

---

2. https://facebook.github.io/jest/

Once Jest finishes its run, it presents you with a prompt:

```
Watch Usage
› Press a to run all tests.
› Press p to filter by a filename regex pattern.
› Press t to filter by a test name regex pattern.
› Press q to quit watch mode.
› Press Enter to trigger a test run.
```

You don't need to choose any of these options: by default, Jest will start running new tests as soon as you add them.

Now that you have installed Jest and verified that you're able to run it, let's write our first test.

Test a Single Function

Testing user interfaces adds noise and complexity, so it's best to test as much as you can without involving the user interface. Putting application logic in functions outside components lets us work more efficiently. In our word counter, we've already extracted the countWords() function and placed it in a separate module:

```
wordcounter/src/countWords.js
function countWords(text) {
  return text ? text.match(/\w+/g).length : 0;
}

export default countWords;
```

This module exports the countWords() function by default. It's a good idea to test this logic on its own, as long as you're testing meaningful functionality instead of implementation details.

Create a new _tests_ directory in the src directory. The directory name must start and end with two underscores to match the regular expression that Jest uses to locate the tests in the project directory. Then create a file named count.test.js in the _tests_ directory. To access the word count function, import the countWords function at the top of count.test.js:

```
wordcounter/src/__tests__/count.test.js
import countWords from '../countWords';
```

Pay attention to the path, as the countWords module is in the parent directory, so you must use two dots before the first slash to access the parent folder.

Now that you've got countWords() in scope, call it and check that its output conforms to what you expect with the it(), describe(), and expect() functions. These functions let you organize your test code and make assertions about the results. If you run test files with Jest, you can use them without importing them. Jest places them in scope automatically. Let's test countWords().

Define individual tests by calling it(). Each test asserts one or more properties of the objects under test with the expect() function. If any of the assertions fails, Jest reports the entire test as failed, so to better understand failures, you'll want to write more tests with fewer assertions per test rather than a few tests with a lot of assertions.

Let's create a test to check that countWords() correctly computes the number of words we pass in. The it() function takes a string describing the test and a callback, which is the actual test. For the callback, you can use either the function keyword or arrow functions; arrow functions are faster to type, so that's what we'll use. In the callback, call expect() to compare the return value of countWords() with the expected result:

```
wordcounter/src/__tests__/count.test.js
it('counts the correct number of words', () => {
  expect(countWords('One two three')).toBe(3);
});
```

This test verifies that countWords() returns 3 when you pass it 'One two three'. We call countWords() and pass its return value to expect(). expect() returns a wrapper with functions that let us check the return value. The function toBe() checks simple values like numbers and strings; it's equivalent to a comparison with the === operator.

If you've still got Jest running in the background, Jest runs the test automatically when you save the file; else, run npm test again. Jest finds your new test and prints something similar to this:

```
PASS   __tests__/count.test.js
 the counting function
   ✓ counts the correct number of words (3ms)

Test Suites: 1 passed, 1 total
Tests:       1 passed, 1 total
Snapshots:   0 total
Time:        1.381s
Ran all test suites related to changed files.
```

The idea behind naming the test function it() is that the test and its output should read like a description of what you're testing. Since Jest prints the test descriptions when you run the tests, descriptive names help you understand what's going on after a test fails. If error messages show up even if the test passes, your code might be generating console warnings. Read the messages to understand what's going on and fix it.

Good tests check edge cases. When the user deletes all the text, countWords() receives an empty string, so we are especially interested in the empty string input. Instead of stuffing a second assertion in the same test, create a separate test. In this way, Jest will report the two cases separately, so you'll know immediately which one of the two has failed.

To make the test output more readable, group related tests in *suites* with the describe() function. describe() takes a string describing the suite and a callback that contains the test code. Suites enhance the test output as Jest groups the results of tests in the same suite. Choose the suite description carefully as Jest will print it on the console to identify the tests. Create a test suite for the wordCount() function inside count.test.js:

wordcounter/src/__tests__/count.test.js
```
➤  describe('the counting function', () => {
      it('counts the correct number of words', () => {
        expect(countWords('One two three')).toBe(3);
      });
➤  });
```

Create a new test within the same suite, but this time pass the empty string to countWords() and ensure you get 0 for the length:

wordcounter/src/__tests__/count.test.js
```
   it('counts the correct number of words', () => {
     expect(countWords('One two three')).toBe(3);
   });

➤  it('counts an empty string', () => {
➤    expect(countWords('')).toBe(0);
➤  });
```

Once again, we call it() with a description for the test case and a callback. Inside the callback, we pass the empty string to countWords() and assert that the result length is 0 with toBe().

When the tests run again, notice that Jest now reports the results of the second test:

```
PASS  __tests__/count.test.js
  the counting function
    ✓ counts the correct number of words (2ms)
    ✓ counts an empty string

Test Suites: 1 passed, 1 total
Tests:       2 passed, 2 total
Snapshots:   0 total
Time:        2.095s
Ran all test suites related to changed files.
```

Now that you've got the hang of creating tests, let's test React components.

Test Component Boundaries

One common pattern that we have used in the word counter is lifting the state into a parent component and updating its children via props. A good way to test is to instantiate the parent component, trigger some events on it, and check whether the children update correctly.

For this type of test, it's enough to render a component and its immediate children. Skipping the creation of the whole DOM structure will speed up the tests considerably. To perform this *shallow rendering*, we'll use a library called Enzyme.[3] We'll construct an element and its immediate children, then simulate the user interaction on the parent, and check that the changes propagate correctly to the children.

Start by installing Enzyme and its dependency as development dependencies:

```
$ npm i --save-dev enzyme react-test-renderer
```

The react-test-renderer library renders React elements to JavaScript objects without depending on the DOM, and Enzyme lets us more easily traverse these objects and make assertions about them.

Let's now test the WordCounter component. We'll create an Editor instance, simulate filling it with text, then check that the word count and progress bar update correctly.

Create a file in the _tests_ directory named WordCounter.test.js. To render Word-Counter, we'll use the shallow() function from Enzyme, instead of ReactDOM.render(). shallow() only renders the component and its immediate children.

To use shallow(), we'll need to create React elements, so import React at the top of WordCounter.test.js. Also import the shallow() function from Enzyme and the WordCounter, Editor, ProgressBar, and Counter components from your own project:

```
wordcounter/src/__tests__/WordCounter.test.js
import React from 'react';
import { shallow } from 'enzyme';
import WordCounter from '../WordCounter';
import countWords from '../countWords';
import Counter from '../Counter';
import Editor from '../Editor';
import ProgressBar from '../ProgressBar';
```

---

3. http://airbnb.io/enzyme/

The Enzyme module exports multiple functions instead of a single default export. To select the import you need, surround the name of the function you wish to import with braces.

Similar to how we tested different arguments for count(), we'll create two separate tests: one for the counter and one for the progress bar. When we test user interfaces, it's easy to get lost in details. Tests should assert something meaningful about the behavior of your application. We'll start by testing the core functionality of our application: we'll check that the counter displays the exact number of words when somebody types in some text. This way, a test failure will indicate that the application doesn't work anymore.

The setup is identical for both tests, so we'll house them both in the same suite and set up the WordCounter only once at the start of the suite. Create a new suite with describe() and use shallow() to render a WordCounter element directly inside the describe() callback:

```
wordcounter/src/__tests__/WordCounter.test.Js
describe('When I type some words', () => {
  const target = 10;
  const inputString = 'One two three four';
  const wordCounter = shallow(<WordCounter targetWordCount={target} />);
});
```

Store the target word count and the input string to be able to check the output later. Create a WordCounter element and pass it to shallow(). Set the targetWordCount prop to the target constant you just declared. Jest automatically reads the .babelrc configuration and applies the required transforms to the test source, so you can use JSX in the test files.

shallow() returns a wrapper that exposes some functions to traverse and manipulate the React elements. Now that we've created a shallow WordCounter element, we'll simulate typing the input string with the simulate() function that Enzyme defines on the wrapper. simulate() calls the event handlers that you defined on the React component, but does not generate real events. It also works with the React event system, so to type some text, we need to use the change event instead of the native browser input event. Nevertheless, it's a good enough substitute if we assume that React itself correctly translates events into calls to the vent handlers. First, retrieve the Editor element. To generate the change event, we then need to access the <textarea> element. But shallow() only renders one level deep, so to access the <textarea> element, we need to render an additional level. We can do this by calling dive() on the Editor wrapper. dive() renders an additional level of elements.

```
wordcounter/src/__tests__/WordCounter.test.js
  const wordCounter = shallow(<WordCounter targetWordCount={target} />);
➤ const textarea = wordCounter.find(Editor).dive().find('textarea');
➤ textarea.simulate('change', { target: { value: inputString } });
});
```

We call find() on the WordCounter wrapper and pass it the Editor component to retrieve all Editor child elements. We know there's only one Editor, so we can assign the return value and use it without further checks. Since <textarea> is a base HTML element, there's no corresponding React component, so retrieve the <textarea> element by passing 'textarea' as a string to find().

simulate() takes an event name as a string. It invokes the event handler corresponding to the event name, with the event data you pass as the second argument. Editor reads the text from the event.target.value property, so pass the text you want to input in the target.value key in the event data.

Once you have simulated typing in the Editor element, create a test to check that the word counter updated correctly. Retrieve the Counter element and check the value of its count prop against the value returned by countWords():

```
wordcounter/src/__tests__/WordCounter.test.js
it('displays the correct count as a number', () => {
  const counter = wordCounter.find(Counter);
  expect(counter.prop('count')).toBe(countWords(inputString));
});
```

As before, we define the test with it(). This time, we pass the Counter component itself to find() to retrieve the Counter element. Another advantage of this method of finding child elements is that the test keeps working if we change the Counter to generate different markup. To check that the Counter element updated correctly, we call prop() on the Counter wrapper to access its count prop. prop() takes a string containing a prop name and returns the corresponding prop value. Showing how the expected value is calculated makes the intent of the test clearer. Calculate the expected value with countWords() and compare it to the count prop value with toBe(). If you run the tests again, Jest reports an additional passing test.

```
PASS  src/__tests__/count.test.js
  the counting function
    ✓ counts the correct number of words (2ms)
    ✓ counts an empty string

Test Suites: 1 passed, 1 total
Tests:       2 passed, 2 total
Snapshots:   0 total
Time:        0.066s, estimated 1s
```

Let's check that the progress bar also updates as expected. Simulating the typing at the start of the WordCounter suite allows us to access the same word-Counter instance with the same state in all tests, so we won't have to repeat the setup. Create a new test in the same suite where you retrieve the ProgressBar element and verify the value of the completion prop. Pass the ProgressBar component to find() to retrieve the ProgressBar element, then check that the completion prop matches the expected value by calling toBe():

```
wordcounter/src/__tests__/WordCounter.test.js
it('displays the correct progress', () => {
  const progressBar = wordCounter.find(ProgressBar);
  expect(progressBar.prop('completion')).toBe(
    countWords(inputString) / target
  );
});
```

Because of shallow rendering, you have to access the props instead of the values in the generated HTML.

To help pinpoint errors, test your application by working through shallow slices of your element tree, manipulating the parent, and checking the immediate children. Some developers write tests to check that triggering a certain input calls a certain internal function. Our approach is better because we check whether components communicate correctly with each other through the same props used in the actual application.

You can now test whether components can pass data around, but sometimes you are more concerned about whether they are rendering the correct UI. Since using detailed assertions about every element becomes very time consuming, we'll speed up the process with snapshots.

Prevent Visual Regressions

If you compose your React applications as we have been doing so far, there's a clear separation between parts of the application that handle logic and parts that just concern themselves with the UI. Checking that the UI matches expectations is tedious. Even if a component outputs different HTML elements, the visual result might turn out to be identical, so tests that check the generated HTML might break even though the application still displays the expected UI. Although these sort of tests tend to break without good reason, you might not want to skip them completely, as they still can alert you that something is wrong. We'll compromise and use a solution that will let you write and update tests very fast, so that you still have some sort of safety net, without spending too much time keeping the tests up to date.

Instead of selecting parts of the UI and comparing them with the expected result by writing code by hand, we can use snapshot tests. Snapshot tests compare a rendered element to a JSON representation of the same element. The first time a snapshot test runs, it's not much of a test, as it just generates the JSON representation. On subsequent test runs, snapshot tests generate a new snapshot and fail whenever they detect a difference with the original snapshot. To see how this works in practice, let's create a snapshot test for the Counter component.

First, we need to install an additional development dependency. To be able to render component snapshots, install react-test-renderer:

```
$ npm i --save-dev react-test-renderer
```

In the _tests_ directory, create a new file named Counter.test.js and import the test renderer, React, and the Counter component:

```
wordcounter/src/__tests__/Counter.test.js
import React from 'react';
import renderer from 'react-test-renderer';
import Counter from '../Counter';
```

Then create a new test suite with one test function. As before, describe() introduces the test suite, and it() sets up a single test.

```
wordcounter/src/__tests__/Counter.test.js
describe('A counter', () => {
  it('Displays the count and label', () => {
  });
});
```

Compare the render output with a snapshot in the body of the it() callback. Create a Counter element, then pass it to renderer.create(). Convert the result to JSON, then use expect() and toMatchSnapshot() to assert that it matches the stored snapshot:

```
wordcounter/src/__tests__/Counter.test.js
describe('A counter', () => {
  it('Displays the count and label', () => {
➤    const counter = renderer.create(<Counter legend="Count" count={34} />);
➤    expect(counter.toJSON()).toMatchSnapshot();

  });
});
```

Jest generates the snapshot during the first run, and by convention, a snapshot test always passes the first time. Right now, there's no snapshot stored yet. To generate the initial snapshot, run the tests:

```
$ npm test
```

When the test completes, Jest informs you it has created one new snapshot:

```
Snapshot Summary
› 1 snapshot written in 1 test suite.

Test Suites: 2 passed, 2 total
Tests:       3 passed, 3 total
Snapshots:   1 added, 1 total
Time:        1.37s
Ran all test suites.
```

If you run the tests again, Jest uses the snapshot it generates in the first test run as a reference. Snapshot tests pass if the result matches the snapshot, so snapshot tests are accurate only if the component rendered correctly when you generated the snapshot. If you need someone else to run the same tests as you, you need to share the _tests_/_snapshots_ directory with them, as Jest stores the snapshots in there.

Let's demonstrate what happens when the component does not match the snapshot. Suppose you want to change the markup of the Counter component to make it more accessible. Open Counter.js and enclose the description in a <label> element and the count in an <output> element:

```
wordcounter/src/Counter.js
function Counter({ count }) {
  return (
➤     <p className="mb2">
➤       <label htmlFor="count">Word count: </label>
➤       <output id="count">
➤         {count}
➤       </output>
➤     </p>
  );
}
```

htmlFor= on <label> points to id= on <output>, making the relationship between <label> and <output> explicit. Let's see how the snapshot tests report the change. Run the tests again:

```
$ npm test
```

The snapshot test fails, since the output changed from when you recorded the snapshot. To help you pinpoint the change causing the failure, Jest prints a diff showing where the new version differs from the old one.

```
FAIL  __tests__/Counter.test.js
  ● A counter › Displays the count and label

    expect(value).toMatchSnapshot()

    Received value does not match stored snapshot 1.
```

```
   - Snapshot
   + Received

   @@ -1,6 +1,11 @@
     <p
       className="text-muted">
   -   Count
   -
   -   34
   +   <label
   +     htmlFor="count">
   +     Count
   +   </label>
   +   <output
   +     id="count">
   +     34
   +   </output>
     </p>
```

Whenever a snapshot test fails, you must examine the diff and decide whether the change was intentional. If the change happened by mistake, fix the problem in the application code until the snapshot test passes again. If you wanted the change, update the snapshot to use the current version as the reference from now on by running the tests with the -u flag:

```
$ npm test -- -u
```

Jest reports that it has updated one snapshot, and all tests pass again:

```
 PASS  __tests__/Counter.test.js
 PASS  __tests__/count.test.js

Snapshot Summary
 › 1 snapshot updated in 1 test suite.
```

You will frequently want to extract separate components from a component that has become very large. In that case, snapshots help you confirm that you preserve the original output. The inconvenient part is that the test fails when any change alters the component's appearance, but that tends to occur in all tests that check a UI. Try to keep your components small, but test all props.

You want to maximize your tests' efficiency, as well as write the least amount of test code to find the most amount of bugs. If the tests break all the time because of implementation details, then they're not supplying very valuable information, because whether they break or not does not tell you that you made a mistake.

What You Learned

Storing logic in separate functions, in addition to giving you more freedom to reorganize your components, makes your code more testable.

To test components, isolate slices of the application with Enzyme and check that props propagate correctly from parent to children.

Snapshots verify that you did not introduce undesired changes into how your React elements render.

Writing good tests forces you to think about the boundaries between components: that is precisely what you need to avoid spreading state everywhere.

Now that you've got testing under your belt, you're ready to tackle more complex architectures. In the next chapter, you will learn how to use the Redux architecture.

CHAPTER 5

Using Redux as a Central Data Store

You learned to share application state by pushing the state to parent components and passing props from parent to child. In this way, the application logic becomes more predictable and you can manage even complex interfaces. However, under some conditions, this model can get in the way. The Redux[1] library provides an additional way to manage an application's state.

Here are a few cases where you might want to consider Redux:

1. You want to move components around and leave the state management code as it is.

2. You want to access state independently of where the element sits in the hierarchy.

3. You want to add elements without affecting the state.

4. You want advanced debugging abilities, because your state transitions are complicated.

5. You want to reuse code for a mobile application. Since Redux separates the state from the components, you can share more code with a React Native[2] application.

If any of these sound interesting to you, you might want to give Redux a try.

As you saw with the word counter example, to share state among many components, you push it up to the parent components. If components are numerous and far apart, you end up pushing all the state to the top of the application. State becomes large, and it gets difficult to keep track of state changes.

---

1. http://redux.js.org/
2. https://facebook.github.io/react-native/

Redux places state outside of components, in a single separate object. A separate library, React Redux,[3] grants any component access to this single object, so you don't have problems passing down props.

While you could come up with your own React and Redux integration, React Redux provides a battle-tested and performant system that allows you to introduce Redux in most React applications with minimal rewrites of existing components. Redux itself is more of a toolkit than a ready-made solution. We'll learn one possible usage. Redux itself is fairly low-level, and you can build a few different styles of solutions with it.

The example application we'll build won't be very complex. In fact, Redux may seem unnecessary; you could do this with just React. However, this will let you focus on the core concepts of Redux and give you a starting point to work with.

We'll build a movie guide that displays movies you can watch this week. The guide organizes movies by day and allows you to mark a movie as a favorite; it activates a filter to show only your favorite movies. Here are the features we'll implement:

- Each movie has a title and a day.
- Each movie is listed under the day it shows on.
- The user interface loads first, then the movies are fetched.
- Users can select each movie in the calendar as a favorite.
- Users can toggle between showing all the movies or only their favorites.

Before we dive into the application, let's start with an overview of how Redux works.

Redux Fundamentals

You can manage some application state without Redux, but everything that Redux manages goes into a single object called the *store*. Unrestricted access to the same state can reintroduce the errors that React's prop system was meant to avoid. We need a system to enforce some constraints so that our application doesn't devolve into a mess.

Redux solves this problem by preventing you from modifying the state directly. Instead, you create *actions*. Actions are similar to events like click and change, but describe high-level events unique to your application. For example, actions could be "Item added to cart" for an ecommerce application, or "Save requested" for a document editor. We'll represent actions with JavaScript objects.

---

3.   https://github.com/reactjs/react-redux

You're in charge of creating action objects and filling them with the information you require to update the state by capturing events like you did in Chapter 2, *Work with State and Events*, on page 17. Once you've defined your actions, you send them to the store by calling store.dispatch() on the store object. The React Redux library calls store.dispatch() for you, so you won't use store.dispatch() as much as without React Redux.

Reducers are the functions that perform state updates. Reducers live inside the store. When you call dispatch(), all reducers receive the action object and determine how to update the state based on the contents of the action. Like actions, you define reducers yourself. Reducers could change the state in place, but in practice, the debugging capabilities and the React Redux library assume that reducers return a new copy of the state for every change. That means you have to construct an entirely new state for every update, even making new copies of fields that remain the same. This is good, though, as it allows you to inspect and replay the state history, which helps you track down bugs. With immutable state, React Redux can also easily determine when to re-render a component: it compares the old with the new state by reference.

Finally, you must map the state to the component props. In a large application, you can extract the code that creates component props from state into their own functions called *selectors*.

The overall flow looks like this:

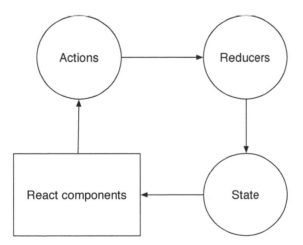

Let's start by building the data layer of our application so you can get familiar with the basic Redux data flow. Then we'll map the data to the user interface with React Redux.

Design the Data Flow

We'll start by analyzing our application so we can figure out how to express its functionality with actions and reducers, and how these actions map to features. Then we'll design the state and use reducers to create updated copies of the state, and we'll examine the behavior of the Redux store in the browser with the Redux development tools, even when you haven't built any user interface yet.

The techniques we'll use might feel a bit odd at first, so initially we won't concern ourselves with the UI so you can focus on the basics of Redux itself. Creating actions and reducers separately from the UI will also demonstrate one of the main features of Redux: keeping the data layer completely decoupled from the structure of the UI.

Let's set up the project structure so we have got a place for our files. Create a new directory named movieguide and copy the package.json and index.html files from the word counter project. We will also use modules, so copy .babelrc and webpack.config.js too.

Often, it's easiest to start with the actions, because they map to features. Each action represents an event that affects the state. In our case, from the list of features, we can extract the following events: MOVIES_LOADED, FILTER_CHANGED, FAVORITED and UNFAVORITED. Then we turn each event into an action, which we represent with an object. Reducers must know which action they've received, so the only required field in the action object is type, which must be one of the string constants we define. Create a new src directory in the project root and define the constants in a file named actions.js in the src. Preface every constant with export so that you can import them in the reducers module you'll create next:

```
movieguide/src/actions.js
export const FILTER_CHANGED = 'FILTER_CHANGED';
export const MOVIES_LOADED = 'MOVIES_LOADED';
export const FAVORITED = 'FAVORITED';
export const UNFAVORITED = 'UNFAVORITED';
```

Once we've defined the actions, we can determine what the state should look like. FILTER_CHANGED must toggle some variable that indicates whether the filter is on or off. MOVIES_LOADED must update an array of movies. FAVORITED and UNFAVORITED must add and remove movies from an array of favorites. The state object will look like this:

```
{ loading, movies, filter, favorites }
```

loading is a boolean variable indicating whether the movie list is loading; movies is an array containing all the current movies; filter is a boolean indicating whether the filter is active; and favorites is an array of the current favorite movies.

Once we've got the shape of the state object, we need to organize our reducers. We'll take a shortcut and use the combineReducers() function that Redux provides. With combineReducers(), each reducer manages a single field in the state object, so we need exactly one reducer function for every field in the state object. We'll define functions for movies(), favorites(), filter(), and loading().

We'll start with the movies() reducer. This reducer responds to the MOVIES_LOADED action and updates the state with the new movies. Create a new file named reducers.js in the src directory and import the action constants you defined in actions.js:

```
movieguide/src/reducers.js
import {
  FILTER_CHANGED,
  MOVIES_LOADED,
  FAVORITED,
  UNFAVORITED
} from './actions';
```

We'll use these constants to identify the actions in the reducers. The reducer examines the current action, and returns the updated state.

Now create the movies() reducer, which manages the movies array in the state object. MOVIES_LOADED is the only action the movies() reducer cares about. When movies() receives the MOVIES_LOADED action, it replaces the current movies with the new ones defined in the action object.

```
movieguide/src/reducers.js
export function movies(state = [], action) {
  switch (action.type) {
    case MOVIES_LOADED:
      return action.movies;
    default:
      return state;
  }
}
```

Since we're inside the movies() reducer, and we'll be using combineReducers(), the state variable represents the movies array. switch executes a different action based on the value of action.type. When action.type is MOVIES_LOADED, we return action.movies to replace the movies array. We generate the actions in our own code, so we must be careful that the structure of our action objects matches what the reducers expect based on the constant we use for the action type field. In all other cases, we want to keep the movies array the same as before, so we return the current state, in the default case. When you use combineReducers(), you must always define the return value, so be sure to set the default value of state. In this case, we set it to an empty array.

Each reducer can respond to one or more actions and more than one reducer can handle the same action. This allows us to extend the application by adding new reducers and actions, without interfering with existing reducers. For example, when we receive the MOVIES_LOADED action, we also want to change the status of the loading indicator, and for that we need to toggle the loading field inside the state. In reducers.js, let's create another reducer called loading() that updates the loading state:

movieguide/src/reducers.js
```
export function loading(state = true, action) {
  switch (action.type) {
    case MOVIES_LOADED:
      return false;
    default:
      return state;
  }
}
```

Here, combineReducers() guarantees that state represents whether the movies are still waiting to load. In this case, we default to true as we're still waiting for the movies to load when the application starts. When action.type is MOVIES_LOADED, return a new state set to false. Since all other actions don't affect the loading state, we return the current state otherwise. Both movies() and loading() respond to the same action but update different parts of the state. This feature allows you to perform additional operations in response to an action without reducers stepping on each other's toes.

Next, let's handle the filter state. Create a new reducer called filter() in reducers.js. This reducer reacts to the FILTER_CHANGED action by replacing the current state with the value of the filter:

movieguide/src/reducers.js
```
export function filter(state = false, action) {
  switch (action.type) {
    case FILTER_CHANGED:
      return action.filter;
    default:
      return state;
  }
}
```

Here, state represents whether the filter is activated. We set the initial filter state to false by passing a default value for the state parameter. When the action type is FILTER_CHANGED, we replace the current state with the value of action.filter; otherwise, we return the current state.

The final reducer handles the favorites. Start by handling the FAVORITE action type:

```
movieguide/src/reducers.js
export function favorites(state = [], action) {
  switch (action.type) {
    case FAVORITED:
      return [...state, action.movieId];
    default:
      return state;
  }
}
```

We set the favorites to an empty array by default. When the action type is FAVORITED, we return a new array containing all the previous favorites and the new favorite movie id that we get from action.movieId. Then we copy the contents of the old array into a new one. The three dots before the state variable, called the spread operator, copy the contents of the state array.

Next, handle the UNFAVORITED action type:

```
movieguide/src/reducers.js
export function favorites(state = [], action) {
  switch (action.type) {
    case FAVORITED:
      return [...state, action.movieId];
➤   case UNFAVORITED:
➤     return state.filter(id => id !== action.movieId);
    default:
      return state;
  }
}
```

filter() takes a function and returns a new array that contains all the elements of the old array, except those for which the function returns false. The function we pass to filter() compares the ids in the state array with action.movieId. It returns false when the id in the state array matches action.movieId, so the new array contains all previous movie ids except for action.movieId.

Once you've written all of the reducers, we can use combineReducers() to combine them into a single reducer and send each reducer the appropriate slice of the state. combineReducers() returns a single reducer, called the root reducer. When the root reducer receives an action, it calls every other reducer and combines the results into a single object.

To access combineReducers(), install the Redux npm package:

```
$ npm i --save redux
```

In reducers.js, import the combineReducers() function:

moviequide/src/reducers.js
```
import { combineReducers } from 'redux';
```

combineReducers() takes an object, where each property maps a slice of the state to a reducer. The object keys determine the names of the state slice managed by the corresponding reducer. Pass all reducers to combineReducers() and export the result:

moviequide/src/reducers.js
```
export default combineReducers({ movies, filter, favorites, loading });
```

We've already decided to name the state properties the same way as the reducers. When you omit the keys, you'll use the reducer function name as the state property name, which makes it easier to remember.

Let's get our application running. For this, we need to create the store.

You create the store by calling the createStore() function on the root reducer. Since we don't have any UI yet, we'll use the Redux development tools to verify our code runs as expected. These come in two parts: a browser extension and an npm module that modifies the store functionality. You can install the browser extension from the Firefox and Chrome extension manager: it's completely separate from your project, and it works on any website that uses Redux.

A mechanism called *middleware* lets you customize how the Redux store works. The development tools npm module is an example of middleware. It modifies the store so that the store logs every action with the browser extension. Middleware can fundamentally alter the way Redux works. That's why we called Redux more of a toolkit. We won't use middleware except for debugging in this chapter, but this will still give you an idea of how to apply different middleware to the store.

In the src directory, create a new file named store.js. To use the development middleware, install the redux-devtools-extension package:

```
$ npm i --save redux-devtools-extension
```

The redux-devtools-extension package exposes a function called devToolsEnhancer() that returns a store middleware. We've got all the ingredients, so create the store in store.js. Import the root reducer from reducers.js, the createStore() function from the Redux package, and the devToolsEnhancer() function from the redux-devtools-extension package. Pass the root reducer and the return value of devToolsEnhancer() to createStore(). Then export the store as a default export:

movieguide/src/store.js
```
import { createStore } from 'redux';
import { devToolsEnhancer } from 'redux-devtools-extension';
import rootReducer from './reducers';

export default createStore(
  rootReducer,
  devToolsEnhancer()
);
```

Now that the store is ready, we can run the application. We're reusing the webpack configuration from the word counter project, so the index.html file you copied from the word counter should work out of the box. Ensure that index.html contains a link to app-bundle.js, which is where our webpack configuration outputs the build results:

movieguide/index.html
```
<script src="app-bundle.js"></script>
```

Next, serve the application in development mode by running:

```
$ npm start
```

We'll check that the store initializes correctly with the Redux developer tools. Search for "Redux DevTools" in the Chrome or Firefox extension manager and install the extension with the same name.[4]

After you've installed the Redux DevTools browser extension, point the browser at the webpack development server. You'll see an icon in the address bar or next to it.

Click the icon or right-click the page and select Redux DevTools. You'll access the Redux debugger. There's a timeline with the dispatched actions to the left and the state change to the right. New elements are highlighted in green, and removals in red. If there's no change, the pane is empty. After loading the page, you'll see one action: @INIT.

---

4.   https://github.com/zalmoxisus/redux-devtools-extension

When you create the store, Redux automatically sends a special action named @INIT. Since we haven't handled @INIT explicitly, every reducer will return the default state. After the reducers process @INIT, the new state looks like this:

```
{
  loading: false,
  movies: [],
  filter: false,
  favorites: []
}
```

Once you've verified that the store initialized correctly, it's time to send it our actions. Let's load the movies in the store. To make the example more realistic, we'll pretend the movies are loaded from a web service. We'll create a function that returns a promise containing the movie list. When the promise completes, we'll send the store the MOVIES_LOADED action. In the src directory, create a new file named movieApi.js and create a new function that simulates loading the movies:

```
movieguide/src/movieApi.js
export function requestMovies() {
  return new Promise(resolve =>
    setTimeout(
      () =>
        resolve([
          { title: 'Rebel without a Cause', date: 'Monday' },
          { title: 'Ghost in the Shell', date: 'Tuesday' },
          { title: 'High Noon', date: 'Monday' }
        ]),
      1000
    )
  );
}
```

In the Promise constructor, we wait one second by calling setTimeout() with a 1000 milliseconds argument. After the timeout expires, we resolve the promise by passing a movie array to resolve(). Each movie in the array is an object with a title and a date.

When requestMovies() returns the movies array, we'll send the MOVIES_LOADED action to the store. dispatch() sends the action to every reducer, which checks its type property and determines how to handle it. In index.js, call dispatch() with the MOVIES_LOADED action. Import requestMovies() and the MOVIES_LOADED constant. Then call requestMovies() and create a new action with the MOVIES_LOADED type:

```
movieguide/src/index.js
import store from './store';
import { requestMovies } from './movieApi';
import { MOVIES_LOADED } from './actions';
requestMovies().then(movies => store.dispatch({ type: MOVIES_LOADED, movies }));
```

Remember that the movies() reducer expects a movies array on the MOVIES_LOADED action. Set the movies property to the movies array in the resolved promise. If you reload the page and check the redux devtools, you'll see the MOVIES_LOADED action.

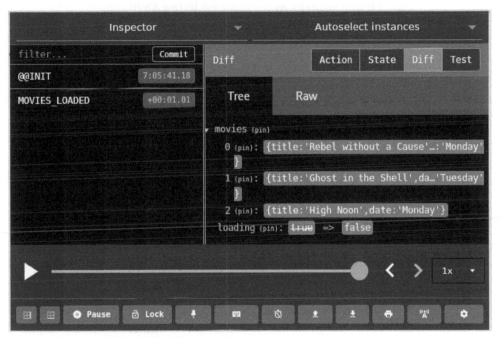

Our movies() reducer will update the state with the new movies. Clicking an action lets you see how the reducers update the state. You can check whether actions are dispatched at all, and whether they result in the right state change. You can also inspect the action payload to dig further.

Of course, making a new copy of the state can be slow. If making copies of the state becomes a bottleneck, you can replace objects and arrays with data structures tuned for making efficient copies, like those in Immutable.js.[5]

You've set up the actions, reducers, and the store, and you've successfully simulated loading the movies in the store from a web service. To work with the rest of the movie guide functionality, we'll need to build the user interface and connect it to the Redux store.

---

5.   https://facebook.github.io/immutable-js/

Connect the User Interface

Our interface will look like this:

Programme

Just favorites ☐

Monday   **Tuesday**

Rebel without a Cause   **Ghost in the Shell**

Favorite ☐   Favorite ☐

High Noon

Favorite ☐

Below each header, we list the movies for that day. While the movies load, we'll display a loading indicator:

Programme

Just favorites ☐

Monday   **Tuesday**

Loading...   Loading...

Some of our components just display the props they receive from their parent, while others talk to the store. To connect the components to the store, we'll use the React Redux library. The advantage of React Redux is that it allows you to transition an existing application to Redux without rewriting most of your components.

The way React Redux works is subtle, so let's break it down. Our React components need to read data from the store so they know what to render. They also need to call the store dispatch() to send actions to the store, and to subscribe() to the store so they know when data has changed. Without React Redux, we would have to repeat this logic for each component that wants to talk to the store. React Redux provides a function called connect(). It creates new wrapper component classes, which you'll sometimes hear people call "higher order components." These handle the process of subscribing to the store, extracting the data your own component wants, and re-rendering your component when the store updates.

Our job will be to create presentational components, then call connect() on them to create the wrapper components that talk to the store. Let's start with the Checkbox component that we'll use both for the filter toggle and the favorite checkbox. In the src directory, create a new file named Checkbox.js and define a function component named Checkbox:

```
movieguide/src/Checkbox.js
import React from 'react';

export default function Checkbox({ checked, onChange, name, label, id }) {
  function onCheck(event) {
    onChange(event.target.checked);
  }

  return (
    <div className="flex mw4">
      <label className="pr2" htmlFor={id}>{label}</label>
      <input
        type="checkbox"
        name={name}
        id={id}
        onChange={onCheck}
        checked={checked}
      />
    </div>
  );
}
```

The checked prop indicates whether the checkbox should be checked. onChange() is an event handler to call when the checkbox checked state changes, and name, label, and id improve accessibility by allowing us to create a label.

This returns an <input> tag with its label. We set the <input> type to *checkbox*. onChecked() calls the onChange() prop with the current checkbox value when the checkbox value changes.

Once we have the Checkbox component, we can immediately create the filter that will toggle whether only favorite movies are displayed. The filter() reducer creates a filter boolean property: when filter is true, only favorite movies are displayed. We need to pass filter as the checked props. The filter() reducer returns a new filter value when the store receives the FILTER_CHANGED action, so we will dispatch the FILTER_CHANGED action when the checkbox value changes.

To get started, install the react-redux package:

```
$ npm i --save react-redux
```

In the src directory, create a new file named Filter.js. Import connect() from react-redux, the FILTER_CHANGED action constant, and finally your own Checkbox component:

movieguide/src/Filter.js
```
import { connect } from 'react-redux';
import { FILTER_CHANGED } from './actions';
import Checkbox from './Checkbox';
```

To pass the store state filter property as the checked prop, define a function named mapStateToProps():

movieguide/src/Filter.js
```
function mapStateToProps(state) {
  return {
    checked: state.filter
  };
}
```

mapStateToProps() receives the current store state. It returns an object. React Redux passes the object as props to Checkbox. To map the state filter property to the checked prop, use state.filter as the value of the checked key.

Next, dispatch the FILTER_CHANGED action when Checkbox calls onChange(). Define a new function, mapDispatchToProps():

movieguide/src/Filter.js
```
function mapDispatchToProps(dispatch) {
  return {
    onChange: filter => {
      dispatch({ type: FILTER_CHANGED, filter });
    }
  };
}
```

mapDispatchToProps() receives the store dispatch() function as an argument. The onChange prop receives the current checkbox value as a boolean. Create a function that takes a boolean and dispatches the FILTER_CHANGED action with the filter property set to the boolean argument. Pass this function as the onChange prop. If you create the same action in multiple places across the application, you can extract the action creation code into its own functions called *action creators*.

Finally, create the wrapper component that talks to the store:

movieguide/src/Filter.js
```
export default connect(mapStateToProps, mapDispatchToProps)(Checkbox);
```

The connect() is a bit weird. It returns a function that returns a component. With the first pair of parentheses, we're calling connect() itself. We pass mapState-ToProps() and mapDispatchToProps(). This returns a function that we can immediately call on the Checkbox component with the second pair of parentheses. The whole thing returns a new component, which renders Checkbox with the props you defined in mapStateToProps() and mapDispatchToProps(). We export this new component so we can use it in the main UI.

Now let's render the filter. In index.js, insert the filter in the UI. Import React, ReactDOM, and the Provider component from React Redux, as well as your own Filter component. To pass the store to the filter component, wrap the whole interface in the Provider component and set the Provider store prop to the store. This will make the store available to all components created with connect() without the need to pass it yourself. In ReactDOM.render(), render the filter component. Pass the control name, id, and label as props:

movieguide/src/index.js
```
import React from 'react';
import ReactDOM from 'react-dom';
import { Provider } from 'react-redux';
import store from './store';
import { requestMovies } from './movieApi';
import { MOVIES_LOADED } from './actions';
import Filter from './Filter';

requestMovies().then(movies => store.dispatch({ type: MOVIES_LOADED, movies }));
ReactDOM.render(
  <Provider store={store}>
    <main className="ph6 pv4">
      <h1 className="mt0">Programme</h1>
      <Filter name="filter" id="filter" label="Just favorites" />
    </main>
  </Provider>,
  document.getElementById('app')
);
```

To serve the application, make sure that index.html contains a <div> with an id of app. Include Tachyons for styling:

movieguide/index.html
```
  <link rel="stylesheet"
    href="https://unpkg.com/tachyons@4.8.0/css/tachyons.min.css"/>
</head>
<body class="sans-serif">
  <div id="app"></div>
```

If webpack-dev-server still runs, reload the page. Otherwise, restart webpack-dev-server with npm start. When you visit the page, the checkbox appears:

Check and uncheck the checkbox a few times, then, with the devtools, inspect the actions you generated. Observe both the dispatched actions and the state snapshots. The FILTER_CHANGED appears in the action list, while the state diff shows the filter property switching between true and false.

We're done with the filter. Let's tackle displaying the movies. We'll build the loading indicator, the movie box, and the list of movie boxes.

Let's start with the loading indicator. Like the filter property, we have a single loading boolean in the store state that indicates whether the movies are still loading or not. The loading indicator component takes a boolean loading prop and a list of children. If loading is true, it displays the children; otherwise, it displays the "Loading…" message. Create the LoadingIndicator component in a file named LoadingIndicator in the src directory:

movieguide/src/LoadingIndicator.js

```
import React from 'react';
import { connect } from 'react-redux';

function LoadingIndicator({ loading, children }) {
  if (loading) {
    return <div>Loading…</div>;
  } else {
    return (
      <div>
        {children}
      </div>
    );
  }
}
```

React passes the children prop implicitly every time an element is a parent of other elements.

Connect the loading prop to the loading property in the store state. In LoadingIndicator.js, create a new mapStateToProps() function:

movieguide/src/LoadingIndicator.js

```
function mapStateToProps(state) {
  return {
    loading: state.loading
  };
}
```

As before, the state parameter represents the store state. We set the loading property to state.loading to pass the loading store state property as the loading prop.

Finally, create the wrapper component. Since we don't need to dispatch any actions, we use connect(), which we imported from React Redux, and pass just mapStateToProps() and LoadingIndicator and export the result:

movieguide/src/LoadingIndicator.js
```
export default connect(mapStateToProps)(LoadingIndicator);
```

Next, create the box to display a single movie. Each box displays the movie title and a checkbox. When the user checks the checkbox, dispatch the FAVORITED action to the store, and dispatch the UNFAVORITED action when the user unchecks the checkbox. In the src directory, create a new file named MovieBox.js and define a new MovieBox component:

movieguide/src/MovieBox.js
```
function MovieBox({ movie, favorite, onFavorite, onUnfavorite }) {
  function onChange(checked) {
    if (checked) {
      onFavorite(movie.title);
    } else {
      onUnfavorite(movie.title);
    }
  }

  return (
    <div className="h4 mt3 pa3 flex flex-column justify-between ba b--dashed">
      <h3 className="mt0 mb3">{movie.title}</h3>
      <Checkbox
        name="addToFavorite"
        id="addToFavorite"
        label="Favorite"
        checked={favorite}
        onChange={onChange}
      />
    </div>
  );
}
```

The movie prop describes the movie to show, favorited indicates whether the user has already favorited the movie, onFavorite is a function to call when the user favorites a movie, and onUnfavorite is a function to call when the user unfavorites a movie. For the interface, import Checkbox. Display the movie title in a header, next to a checkbox with the "Favorite" label. Check the checkbox when favorite is true. Pass onChange() as the onChange prop to Checkbox. onChange() receives the checkbox state as a boolean. If the checkbox is checked, call onFavorite() with the movie id to signal that the user favorited the current movie; else, call onUnfavorite().

Next, we'll use connect() to construct a new component that receives the movies directly from the store and dispatches the FAVORITED and UNFAVORITED actions when the user interacts with the checkbox.

Import the connect() function and the FAVORITED and UNFAVORITED action constants at the top of MovieBox.js:

movieguide/src/MovieBox.js
```
import React from 'react';
import { connect } from 'react-redux';
import Checkbox from './Checkbox';
import { FAVORITED, UNFAVORITED } from './actions';
```

Let's start by mapping the store state to the MovieBox props. The parent component will pass the movie itself, so we only need to pass the favorited state from the store:

movieguide/src/MovieBox.js
```
function mapStateToProps(state, ownProps) {
  return {
    favorite: state.favorites.includes(ownProps.movie.title)
  };
}
```

The second parameter to mapStateToProps() represents the props you pass to the component returned by connect(). To determine whether the movie is favorited, check that the array of favorited movies includes the movie that MovieBox displays. The includes() array function returns true if the array contains the item you pass to includes().

Next, let's map dispatch(). Create another function named mapDispatchToProps():

movieguide/src/MovieBox.js
```
function mapDispatchToProps(dispatch) {
  return {
    onFavorite: movieId => dispatch({ type: FAVORITED, movieId }),
    onUnfavorite: movieId => dispatch({ type: UNFAVORITED, movieId })
  };
}
```

We pass a function that dispatches the FAVORITED action as the onFavorite prop and a function that dispatches the UNFAVORITE action as the onUnfavorite prop.

Finally, create the wrapper component. Pass mapStateToProps() and mapDispatch-ToProps() to connect() and export the result by default:

movieguide/src/MovieBox.js
```
export default connect(mapStateToProps, mapDispatchToProps)(MovieBox);
```

Finally, create the component that lists the movie boxes. In the src directory, create a new file named MovieList.js. The MovieList component displays either a list of movies or the loading indicator. Import MovieBox and LoadingIndicator. The movies prop is an array of movie objects. For each movie object, create a MovieBox element. Assign the MovieBox list to movieBoxes. Place the movie date in the header. Wrap a LoadingIndicator element around the MovieBox list:

movieguide/src/MovieList.js

```
import React from 'react';
import { connect } from 'react-redux';
import MovieBox from './MovieBox';
import LoadingIndicator from './LoadingIndicator';

function MovieList({ movies, date }) {
  const movieBoxes = movies.map(movie =>
    <li key={movie.title}><MovieBox movie={movie} /></li>
  );
  return (
    <div className="w5 pr3">
      <h2>{date}</h2>
      <LoadingIndicator>
        <ol className="list pa0">
          {movieBoxes}
        </ol>
      </LoadingIndicator>
    </div>
  );
}
```

You already connected LoadingIndicator to the store, so that it displays the loading message when the store state loading property is true.

Create mapStateToProps() to retrieve the movies props from the movies property in the store state. The movies to display depend on the filter; if state.filter is true, pass only the favorited movies to the component; else, pass all movies. You also need to filter the movies by date. Access the date for the current MovieList element from ownProps.date:

movieguide/src/MovieList.js

```
function mapStateToProps(state, ownProps) {
  if (state.filter) {
    const activeMovies = state.movies.filter(movie =>
      state.favorites.includes(movie.title)
    );
    return {
      movies: activeMovies.filter(movie => movie.date === ownProps.date)
    };
```

```
    } else {
      return {
        movies: state.movies.filter(movie => movie.date === ownProps.date)
      };
    }
}
```

Finally, pass mapStateToProps() and MovieList to connect() and export the result:

moviequide/src/MovieList.js
```
export default connect(mapStateToProps)(MovieList);
```

Let's render the remaining part of the interface. Open index.js again and import MovieList. For each day, create a MovieList element and pass the day as the date prop. Each MovieList element needs a unique key= prop so that React can render it correctly. Use the day for that. map() returns an array of MovieList elements. Assign it to the movieLists variable, then render each MovieList by placing the whole array inside braces in the JSX structure:

moviequide/src/index.js
```
import React from 'react';
import ReactDOM from 'react-dom';
import { Provider } from 'react-redux';
import store from './store';
import { requestMovies } from './movieApi';
import { MOVIES_LOADED } from './actions';
➤ import MovieList from './MovieList';
import Filter from './Filter';

requestMovies().then(movies => store.dispatch({ type: MOVIES_LOADED, movies }));
➤ const movieLists = ['Monday', 'Tuesday'].map(date =>
➤   <MovieList key={date} date={date} />
➤ );
ReactDOM.render(
    <Provider store={store}>
      <main className="ph6 pv4">
        <h1 className="mt0">Programme</h1>
        <Filter name="filter" id="filter" label="Just favorites" />
➤       <div className="flex flex-row">
➤         {movieLists}
➤       </div>
      </main>
    </Provider>,
    document.getElementById('app')
);
```

Visit the page again, and check that everything works. As you click the filter initially, all of the movies disappear, but if you select one of the movies, it remains. If something misbehaves, check that the FAVORITED and UNFAVORITED actions appear in the Redux devtools. You can also look at the state snapshots and check that the movie titles get added to the favorites.

If you want to develop this application further, you could try extracting action creators and selectors in their own functions.

What You Learned

You can use Redux instead of the built-in setState() if you need a lot of flexibility or if you need to pass the same data to many far-apart components. With Redux, deeply nested or far-apart elements can affect the application state without passing props down many layers of elements.

Redux places the state in a single object called the store. You generate state changes by creating action objects and sending them to the store. React Redux wraps plain presentational components into higher-order components that talk to the store. You can use it both on custom components and to connect existing components to the store.

Redux is a toolkit. You've seen one of the most common ways to use it with React. Middleware can modify Redux behavior extensively, but we've just used middleware to inspect actions at runtime.

We're almost at the end of our journey. Next, we'll learn how to interoperate with different libraries that require direct DOM access.

CHAPTER 6

Work Well with Others

You've seen how to build all-in-one applications, but there's other code out there, as well as developers who don't use React. You'll learn how to publish your code so that other developers can use it as a standalone library without knowing React. Then you'll solve the reverse problem: how to integrate Java-Script code that directly modifies the DOM with React components. Finally, you'll look at the data layer of your application. You've seen how to use setState() and Redux, but another popular technique uses special objects designed to emit events when their contents change. We're going to look at the Backbone.js library and how we can build a React interface on top of existing Backbone models, while keeping the Backbone models and the existing UI working.

Share Your Code with Others

The word counter we've built in the previous chapter executes as soon as the page loads. It'd be easier to integrate it in another application if we could decide when and where the word counter appears, without knowing how React works. To let others without React knowledge use your components in their own application, let's adapt the webpack configuration to make the word counter a library.

If another developer wants to use your word counter library, they will probably expect to access the word counter through the Wordcounter global variable. They'd then assume that calling init() should create the word counter on the element with *app* id=. However, because of how things currently work, this will fail.

Try this out yourself so you can see it in action. In your word counter directory, place the following code in a new file named initialize.js:

```
wordcounter/initialize.js
Wordcounter.init(
  document.getElementById('app')
);
```

Then create a new HTML index page, name it index-library.html, and include initial-ize.js in a <script> tag before the closing <body> tag:

wordcounter/index-library.html

```
<script src="initialize.js"></script>
```

As you load the page and open the console, you'll see the following error:

```
Uncaught ReferenceError: Wordcounter is not defined
```

Let's change how we package our word counter to fix this.

First, let's create a new entry point for our code, so that developers can call a function on a DOM node to create a word counter on that node. Create a new file in the src directory and name it index-library.js.

In this file, export two functions: an init() function that takes a DOM element and initializes the word counter on that element, and a destroy() function to remove the word counter from the page. Import React, ReactDOM, and the WordCounter component:

wordcounter/src/index-library.js

```
import React from 'react';
import ReactDOM from 'react-dom';
import WordCounter from './WordCounter';

export function init(element, target = 10) {
  ReactDOM.render(<WordCounter targetWordCount={target} />, element);
}
export function destroy(element) {
  ReactDOM.unmountComponentAtNode(element);
}
```

init() takes a DOM element and a target word count and renders a WordCounter element on the DOM element. destroy() takes a DOM element and calls React-DOM.unmountComponentAtNode() to remove the editor from that node. We export each function separately.

Now we have two new entry points that let the user choose when and where to instantiate the word counter. Now we have to let users call our new functions through a global variable. webpack will take care of that part. Copy your existing webpack configuration to a new file named webpack.config.library.js. Open the new file and modify the entry point to point to index-library.js:

wordcounter/webpack.config.library.js

```
module.exports = {
  entry: ['./src/index-library.js'],
```

Next, make init() and destroy() available on a global variable. In the output section, set libraryTarget to 'var', and set library to the name of the global variable—in this case, 'WordCounter'. To distinguish the library bundle from the application, change the output file name to library-bundle.js:

```
wordcounter/webpack.config.library.js
output: {
  path: __dirname,
  filename: 'library-bundle.js',
  libraryTarget: 'var',
  library: 'Wordcounter'
},
```

Now that we've made the necessary changes to the webpack configuration, create a new entry in package.json to run webpack with the new configuration. Open package.json and in the scripts section, insert the following script with the library:build key:

```
wordcounter/package.json
    "library:build":
"cross-env NODE_ENV=production webpack -p --config webpack.config.library.js",
```

This code runs webpack, but instead of using the default configuration webpack.config.js, it uses webpack.config.library.js.

To test, run:

```
$ npm run library:build
```

When run, webpack outputs the library bundle to library-bundle.js.

Include library-bundle.js in index-library.html just above initialize.js:

```
wordcounter/index-library.html
➤ <script src="library-bundle.js"></script>
  <script src="initialize.js"></script>
```

Reload the page. Since the WordCounter variable is now defined and contains the init() function, initialize.js manages to create the word counter.

With these changes, a developer who's never heard of React can use the word counter, but if they use many of your components on the same page, the total file size will be huge, because we're including the whole of React in every bundle. It would be more efficient to take React out of the components we distribute, and tell our fellow developer to load React on the page once via a separate <script> tag. Let's make this possible by tweaking the webpack configuration a little more.

To exclude React and ReactDOM from the bundle, add a new section named externals below output in webpack.config.library.js. We'll assume that the libraries will be available as global variables named React and ReactDOM, respectively:

```
wordcounter/webpack.config.library.js
externals: {
  react: 'React',
  'react-dom': 'ReactDOM'
},
```

We use the module name as the key, and the global variable name as the value. Here, the module name is react-dom, and the global variable name is ReactDOM.

Rebuild the library bundle:

```
$ npm run library:build
```

When the build completes, notice the file size of library-bundle.js has gone down quite a bit.

The new library bundle assumes that the React and ReactDOM global variables will exist on the page. Link React and ReactDOM from the CDN. In this case, use the links to the production versions of React and ReactDOM. As you learned in Chapter 1, *An Introduction to Components*, on page 1, you should avoid the development versions in production because they run much slower. Insert the two <script> tags before the library bundle, and reload the page.

```
wordcounter/index-library.html
➤ <script src="https://unpkg.com/react@15/dist/react.min.js"></script>
➤ <script src="https://unpkg.com/react-dom@15/dist/react-dom.min.js"></script>
➤ <script src="library-bundle.js"></script>
<script src="initialize.js"></script>
```

Now the word counter library works fine with React from the CDN.

Now you can distribute your React code so that others can use it in almost any web page. Next, let's see how you can use almost any JavaScript code in your React apps.

Integrate Legacy Widgets

A lot of existing front-end code manipulates DOM nodes directly. It might cost too much time and effort to rewrite this code in React, but by wrapping this code in a React component, you can combine it with other React components without having to rewrite all the UI logic.

As an example, we're going to build a React wrapper for the Pikaday date picker (https://github.com/dbushell/Pikaday) as shown in the figure on page 89.

React date pickers exist already, but the same techniques we'll use to integrate Pikaday will let you wrap any code that accesses the DOM, so you can recycle any of your more exotic widgets.

Pikaday

A refreshing JavaScript Datepicker

Pikaday source on GitHub

Date:

January 2017

Mon Tue Wed Thu Fri Sat Sun

14   15

16   17   18   19   20   21   22

23   24   25   26   27   28   29

30   31

Create a new directory called datepicker-integration. Copy webpack.config.js, package.json, index.html, and .babelrc from the word counter project. Then install Pikaday and React from npm:

```
$ npm i --save pikaday react react-dom babel-preset-react-app
```

We'll create a date picker component in React that uses Pikaday under the hood to avoid re-creating the logic to draw the calendar. Pikaday creates the date picker widget on top of an existing <input> element, but you must pass a real <DOM> node to Pikaday. Unfortunately, React components only return React elements. To work around this limitation, we'll output an <input> element in our component's render() function, wait for React to create the <input> DOM node, obtain a reference to the DOM node, and create the date picker on top of it.

To access the DOM node that React creates, you'll need to use functions that are only defined for class components. In your new project, create a src directory with a new file called DatePicker.js and import React and Pikaday. Then create a new class component called DatePicker:

datepicker-integration/src/DatePicker.js
```
import React from 'react';
import Pikaday from 'pikaday';

class DatePicker extends React.Component {
```

Pikaday will do all the work of displaying the calendar and we just need to create an <input> element. In the render() function, return an <input> element:

datepicker-integration/src/DatePicker.js

```
class DatePicker extends React.Component {
  render() {
    return (
      <input
      />
    );
  }
}
export default DatePicker;
```

Let's test that the <input> field displays. Create an HTML skeleton in index.html that includes app-bundle.js in a <script> at the bottom of the page, or copy the index.html file from the word counter project. Next, create the JavaScript entry point. Inside the src directory, create a new file named index.js and import React, ReactDOM, and the date picker component, then call ReactDOM.render() to insert a date picker element on the element with the id of app:

datepicker-integration/src/index.js

```
import React from 'react';
import ReactDOM from 'react-dom';
import DatePicker from './DatePicker';

ReactDOM.render(<DatePicker />, document.getElementById('app'));
```

Compile and serve the app to check that the <input> element displays:

```
$ npm start
```

Then visit the address that webpack prints on the console. If the page is empty, make sure index.html references app-bundle.js in a <script> tag at the bottom of the page.

Now let's display the date picker. We'll access the DOM node that React generates and pass it to Pikaday to create the date picker. To access the DOM node, we'll use a special prop that React defines on all React elements that correspond to a single HTML element. The ref prop is a function that takes a single parameter. When React creates the DOM node for a React element that represents a simple HTML tag (so not a component), it invokes the ref prop with the DOM node as its argument. React also invokes the ref function a second time: when it destroys the DOM node, it passes null as an argument. Name the argument input and assign it to an instance variable so we can access it later:

datepicker-integration/src/DatePicker.js

```
render() {
  return (
    <input
      ref={input => {
```

```
        this.el = input;
      }}
    />
  );
}
```

this.el now contains a reference to the real DOM node that React creates for the <input> element. To determine whether React is mounting or destroying the node, we'll rely on special functions available in class components. If you create a function named componentDidMount() in a React class component, React will invoke it after it creates the DOM node for the component. Since the DOM node exists when componentDidMount() runs, we'll initialize Pikaday there.

Instance variables are available to any function in the class, so you can access this.el from componentDidMount(). Although this.el can either be the DOM node or null, in componentDidMount() it's going to be the DOM node, so you can pass this.el to the Pikaday constructor. Call Pikaday() in componentDidMount() to initialize the date picker:

datepicker-integration/src/DatePicker.js
```
componentDidMount() {
  const el = this.el;
  const { onSelect } = this.props;
  this.picker = new Pikaday({
    field: el,
    onSelect
  });
}
```

Pikaday() takes an object as the initial configuration. Pass this.el as the field value to initialize the date picker on the <input> element generated by our React component. Rebuild the application and visit the web page. Click inside the <input> field to let the date picker pop up.

To improve the look and feel, grab pikaday.css from the css folder in the GitHub repository (https://github.com/dbushell/Pikaday) and link it at the top of the page.

datepicker-integration/index.html
```
  <link rel="stylesheet" href="src/pikaday.css"/>
</head>
```

By wrapping the Pikaday date picker in a React component, we can combine the date picker with other React components just like any other component we would have written ourselves. However, there's another issue we still need to handle. Sometimes React removes elements from a tree, like when a component renders different elements when its props change. Right now, because of how our component works with Pikaday, every time React destroys the DatePicker element, some stray DOM nodes linger at the bottom of the page.

Let's observe what happens when we remove the date picker component from the page. React provides a function to remove an element directly: React-DOM.unmountComponentAtNode(). Open index.js and use a timeout to remove the React component after three seconds:

datepicker-integration/src/index.js
```
setTimeout(() => {
  ReactDOM.unmountComponentAtNode(document.getElementById('app'));
}, 3000);
```

setTimeout() takes a function as its first argument and a time expressed in milliseconds as its second argument. When the time expires, it executes the ReactDOM.unmountComponentAtNode() function. ReactDOM.unmountComponentAtNode() takes a DOM node as an argument and removes the React element from that node. Open the browser developer tools by right-clicking the page and selecting Inspect, and notice that a <div> that Pikaday created stays at the bottom of the page even after the date picker gets destroyed. It looks like this:

```
<div style="position: static; left: auto; top: auto;"
     class="pika-single is-hidden is-bound">
</div>
```

The markup is still there, together with the event handlers that Pikaday created to open and close the date picker. If we don't clean up, it will consume memory and the performance will degrade if it continues to happen for elements that often get created and deleted, so let's learn how to handle elements that need special cleanup after React unmounts them.

We need to add functionality to the DatePicker component to perform additional actions after its removal. Pikadate provides a destroy() function to remove any trace of the date picker, but we need to call it at the right moment. In a class component, React calls the function componentWillUnmount() just before it removes the DOM node from the page. In the DatePicker component, create componentWillUnmount(). this.picker contains a reference to the Pikaday date picker, so call destroy() on the date picker to remove it:

datepicker-integration/src/DatePicker.js
```
componentWillUnmount() {
  this.picker.destroy();
}
```

Reload the application and notice that now the bottom <div> disappears together with the date picker.

React only takes care of setting up and tearing down our date picker. Pikaday continues to handle all user interaction. This method wraps an existing widget in a React component so that you can keep reusing older code in your React application.

Now you know how to use refs to grab references to DOM nodes, componentDidMount() to manipulate the DOM nodes after React creates them, and componentWillUnmount() to perform any cleanup. With these tools, you'll be able to handle most UI code that was not created with React in mind.

We'll now switch from the view to the model layer, and learn how to integrate a library that manages data differently than what React expects.

Combine React Views with External Models

Backbone (http://backbonejs.org) is a popular library to manage the model layer in JavaScript application. Backbone models are objects that emit events when you modify them. This system works backwards compared to React, where you explicitly call setState() to trigger the updates. Backbone also has its own view utilities, but I want to focus on reusing your Backbone models when you migrate to React as the view. How do you proceed? You'll use a smart container component that manages the Backbone models and two dumb components that display the data and handle user input. This way most of your React components don't contain Backbone-specific code, and you centralize in a single component handling the events emitted by Backbone collections and models.

To demonstrate this approach, you'll build a little interface that displays a list of contacts and allows the user to add new ones. Make a new directory for this example; to build this project, reuse webpack.config.js, package.json, .babelrc, and index.html from the previous examples.

First, we'll build our presentational components. Start with the component to display a contact called ContactCard. ContactCard knows nothing about Backbone. It just takes its data from its contact prop. contact is a plain JavaScript object, with a name, address, and zip property. The component manages no state of its own and doesn't require lifecycle hooks, so create a function component in ContactCard.js in the src directory:

```
backbone-example/src/ContactCard.js
import React from 'react';

function ContactCard({ contact }) {
  return (
    <dl>
      <dt>Name</dt>
      <dd>{contact.name}</dd>
      <dt>Address</dt>
      <dd>{contact.address}</dd>
```

```
        <dt>Post code/ ZIP code</dt>
        <dd>{contact.zip}</dd>
      </dl>
    );
}

export default ContactCard;
```

Next, create a component that displays the whole list called ContactList that creates a new ContactCard element for each of the contacts in its own props. ContactList doesn't know about Backbone either. Its contacts prop is a plain JavaScript array of plain objects. Create ContactList in a file named ContactList.js in the src directory:

backbone-example/src/ContactList.js
```
import React from 'react';
import ContactCard from './ContactCard';

function ContactList({ contacts }) {
  const contactCards = contacts.map(contact =>
    <ContactCard contact={contact} key={contact.cid} />
  );
  return (
    <div>
      <h1>Contacts</h1>
      {contactCards}
    </div>
  );
}

export default ContactList;
```

We use map() to create an array of ContactCard elements.

For the new contact form, first create a TextInput component. This will prevent duplication when you create the form to handle the contact fields. TextInput accepts two props: the input label text and a function that fires when the <input> field changes, to notify TextInput's parent component about the new data.

backbone-example/src/TextInput.js
```
import React from 'react';

function TextInput({ label, changed }) {
  return (
    <label>
      {label}
      <input onChange={changed} />
    </label>
  );
}

export default TextInput;
```

Then assemble the input fields into a ContactForm component. Create a new file in the src directory named ContactForm.js. The constructor initializes a form object to store the form data. save() will be called when the user clicks the submit button and delegates to the onSubmit() function handed in by the parent component.

backbone-example/src/ContactForm.js
```
import React from 'react';
import TextInput from './TextInput';

class ContactForm extends React.Component {
  constructor() {
    super();
    this.form = {};
    this.save = this.save.bind(this);
  }

  save() {
    this.props.onSubmit(this.form);
  }
}

export default ContactForm;
```

Add an update() function that takes a string and returns a new function that updates that particular key in a form object that's part of the component instance. This saves some code duplication when we handle the input fields changes. If you need to create a lot of forms, you can take a look at dedicated libraries like formsy-react (https://github.com/christianalfoni/formsy-react).

backbone-example/src/ContactForm.js
```
update(key) {
  return function(event) {
    this.form[key] = event.target.value;
  }.bind(this);
}

render() {
  return (
    <form>
      <h2>Add contact</h2>
      <TextInput label="Name" changed={this.update('name')} />
      <TextInput label="Address" changed={this.update('address')} />
      <TextInput label="ZIP" changed={this.update('zip')} />
      <TextInput label="Email" changed={this.update('email')} />
      <button type="button" onClick={this.save}>Save</button>
    </form>
  );
}
```

This form component takes a single prop, a function that gets called with this.form as an argument when the user submits the form. The parent component receives the form data and can do what it wants with it.

That's it for the presentational components. Now let's define the Backbone models. You can install the latest Backbone version from npm:

```
$ npm i --save backbone
```

You'll also need to install jQuery, a Backbone dependency:

```
$ npm i --save jquery
```

The Backbone package exports a single Backbone object. Backbone.Model.extend() creates a new Backbone model. Create a minimal Backbone model that represents a single contact:

backbone-example/src/Contact.js
```
import Backbone from 'backbone';

const Contact = Backbone.Model.extend({});

export default Contact;
```

We'll leave the arguments for the model empty as we don't need to add any methods to the model for this example. You can continue to use all of Backbone's Model facilities to perform validation and fetch data if that's practical for you. You'll also need a collection. Backbone collections store lists of models. In ContactCollection.js, create a minimal Backbone collection that expects a model type of Contact. Specifying the model type allows you to turn plain JSON objects added to the collection into Contact instances automatically.

backbone-example/src/ContactCollection.js
```
import Backbone from 'backbone';
import Contact from './Contact';

const ContactCollection = Backbone.Collection.extend({
  model: Contact
});

export default ContactCollection;
```

Finally, build the container component to manage the Backbone collection. In the src directory, create a new class component named App and initialize its state to an empty array:

backbone-example/src/App.js
```
class App extends React.Component {
  constructor(props) {
    super(props);
```

```
    this.state = { data: [] };
  }
}
```

To retrieve the form data, create a function that takes an object and adds it
to the collection:

backbone-example/src/App.js
```
addElement(item) {
  this.props.collection.add(item);
}
```

To access props in the constructor, you need to define a props parameter and
pass it to super(). this.props.collection points to a ContactCollection you will pass to
the App element as a prop. item is a plain JavaScript object. Since we defined
the model property when we created the ContactCollection collection type, add()
automatically converts item to a Contact instance. Backbone collections emit
the add event when you add an item. When add fires, call a function that
updates the App's component state with the new contents of the collection. In
this way, you make use of the normal React rendering mechanism. When a
new item gets added to the collection, replace the current state with the collection contents.

backbone-example/src/App.js
```
constructor(props) {
  super(props);
  this.state = { data: [] };
➤ this.addElement = this.addElement.bind(this);
➤ this.props.collection.on('add', () => {
➤   this.setState(() => ({ data: this.props.collection.toJSON() }));
➤ });
}
```

Despite its name, toJSON() returns an array of plain JavaScript objects. Remember
to call bind() on addElement() so this keeps pointing to the App component.

In the render() function, pass addElement() as the onSubmit prop to ContactForm.

backbone-example/src/App.js
```
render() {
  return (
    <div>
      <ContactList contacts={this.state.data} />
      <ContactForm onSubmit={this.addElement} />
    </div>
  );
}
```

ContactForm calls addElement() with the contents of the form as a simple object; it's handy that add() also accepts JSON objects instead of Backbone.Model instances.

We've got both the Backbone models and the React components ready, so let's run our application. We'll start with an empty contact list. In index.js, render the App element with a new empty ContactCollection:

```
backbone-example/src/index.js
import ReactDOM from 'react-dom';
import React from 'react';
import ContactCollection from './ContactCollection';
import App from './App';

const collection = new ContactCollection();

ReactDOM.render(
  <App collection={collection} />,
  document.getElementById('app')
);
```

Let's run the application. Run

```
$ npm start
```

and visit the application in your web browser.

Contacts

Add contact

Name Jane Eyre	Address	ZIP	Email	Save

Fill in the form and click Save to add a new contact.

Listening to the change event allows the App component to re-render even if a legacy Backbone view modifies the collection.

Limit Backbone-specific code to the top component and do not listen for model changes across all your components. Subscribe to model events in the top component and update this.state whenever the model changes. This will limit event-spaghetti, where events are firing from all over the place and you cannot trace the interaction that triggered them. Use toJSON() to get your data as plain JavaScript objects in this.state and pass it to the other components via props. As you deal with plain JavaScript data structures, your code is more readable and allows you to eventually move away from Backbone completely.

What You Learned

You can now share your React components with others who don't use React, and you can integrate other frameworks in a React application. You learned how to access the DOM directly to reuse prebuilt widgets, and you combined Backbone with React props to use Backbone models as the source of data for your app.

You now have enough React practice to tackle a wide range of challenges. Try a larger project from start to finish. You could prototype an application you've had in mind for some time, or apply your knowledge to a project at work. Be sure to refer to React's official documentation[1] for guidance.

If you're responsible for styling the application, tools that let you place styles inside React components[2] can help you refactor with more confidence. Prebuilt component sets like Rebass[3] let you create standard layouts much quicker.

Finally, if you regularly build large applications, consider learning TypeScript.[4] TypeScript is a superset of JavaScript that adds static types to the language. Static types let you spot many errors before the application runs. They're also useful for ensuring your component props are typed correctly.

Front-end development keeps changing at a rapid pace; I hope that reading this book helped you rethink how you go about designing web applications and gave you some ideas you can take with you beyond React.

---

1.   https://facebook.github.io/react/
2.   https://www.styled-components.com/
3.   http://jxnblk.com/rebass/
4.   https://www.typescriptlang.org/

Bibliography

[AS96]   Harold Abelson and Gerald Jay Sussman. *Structure and Interpretation of Computer Programs*. MIT Press, Cambridge, MA, 2nd, 1996.

The Modern Web

Get up to speed on the latest JavaScript techniques.

Deliver Audacious Web Apps with Ember 2

It's time for web development to be fun again, time to write engaging and attractive apps – fast – in this brisk tutorial. Build a complete user interface in a few lines of code, create reusable web components, access RESTful services and cache the results for performance, and use JavaScript modules to bring abstraction to your code. Find out how you can get your crucial app infrastructure up and running quickly, so you can spend your time on the stuff great apps are made of: features.

This updated edition covers the 2.12 LTS version of Ember, making the sample project compatible with future releases of Ember and better align with current common practice.

Matthew White
(146 pages) ISBN: 9781680500783. $24
https://pragprog.com/book/mwjsember

Reactive Programming with RxJS

Reactive programming is revolutionary. It makes asynchronous programming clean, intuitive, and robust. Use the RxJS library to write complex programs in a simple way, unifying asynchronous mechanisms such as callbacks and promises into a powerful data type: the Observable. Learn to think about your programs as streams of data that you can transform by expressing *what* should happen, instead of having to painstakingly program *how* it should happen. Manage real-world concurrency and write complex flows of events in your applications with ease.

Sergi Mansilla
(142 pages) ISBN: 9781680501292. $18
https://pragprog.com/book/smreactjs

Secure JavaScript and Web Testing

Secure your Node applications and see how to really test on the web.

Secure Your Node.js Web Application

Cyber-criminals have your web applications in their crosshairs. They search for and exploit common security mistakes in your web application to steal user data. Learn how you can secure your Node.js applications, database and web server to avoid these security holes. Discover the primary attack vectors against web applications, and implement security best practices and effective countermeasures. Coding securely will make you a stronger web developer and analyst, and you'll protect your users.

Karl Düüna
(230 pages) ISBN: 9781680500851. $36
https://pragprog.com/book/kdnodesec

The Way of the Web Tester

This book is for everyone who needs to test the web. As a tester, you'll automate your tests. As a developer, you'll build more robust solutions. And as a team, you'll gain a vocabulary and a means to coordinate how to write and organize automated tests for the web. Follow the testing pyramid and level up your skills in user interface testing, integration testing, and unit testing. Your new skills will free you up to do other, more important things while letting the computer do the one thing it's really good at: quickly running thousands of repetitive tasks.

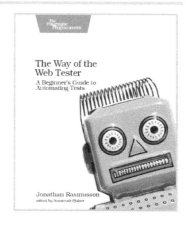

Jonathan Rasmusson
(256 pages) ISBN: 9781680501834. $29
https://pragprog.com/book/jrtest

Pragmatic Programming

We'll show you how to be more pragmatic and effective, for new code and old.

Your Code as a Crime Scene

Jack the Ripper and legacy codebases have more in common than you'd think. Inspired by forensic psychology methods, this book teaches you strategies to predict the future of your codebase, assess refactoring direction, and understand how your team influences the design. With its unique blend of forensic psychology and code analysis, this book arms you with the strategies you need, no matter what programming language you use.

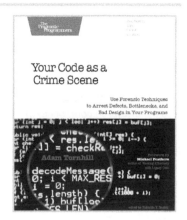

Adam Tornhill
(218 pages) ISBN: 9781680500387. $36
https://pragprog.com/book/atcrime

The Nature of Software Development

You need to get value from your software project. You need it "free, now, and perfect." We can't get you there, but we can help you get to "cheaper, sooner, and better." This book leads you from the desire for value down to the specific activities that help good Agile projects deliver better software sooner, and at a lower cost. Using simple sketches and a few words, the author invites you to follow his path of learning and understanding from a half century of software development and from his engagement with Agile methods from their very beginning.

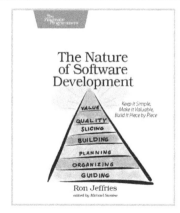

Ron Jeffries
(176 pages) ISBN: 9781941222379. $24
https://pragprog.com/book/rjnsd

The Pragmatic Bookshelf

The Pragmatic Bookshelf features books written by developers for developers. The titles continue the well-known Pragmatic Programmer style and continue to garner awards and rave reviews. As development gets more and more difficult, the Pragmatic Programmers will be there with more titles and products to help you stay on top of your game.

Visit Us Online

This Book's Home Page
https://pragprog.com/book/ljfreact
Source code from this book, errata, and other resources. Come give us feedback, too!

Register for Updates
https://pragprog.com/updates
Be notified when updates and new books become available.

Join the Community
https://pragprog.com/community
Read our weblogs, join our online discussions, participate in our mailing list, interact with our wiki, and benefit from the experience of other Pragmatic Programmers.

New and Noteworthy
https://pragprog.com/news
Check out the latest pragmatic developments, new titles and other offerings.

Save on the eBook

Save on the eBook versions of this title. Owning the paper version of this book entitles you to purchase the electronic versions at a terrific discount.

PDFs are great for carrying around on your laptop—they are hyperlinked, have color, and are fully searchable. Most titles are also available for the iPhone and iPod touch, Amazon Kindle, and other popular e-book readers.

Buy now at *https://pragprog.com/coupon*

Contact Us

Online Orders:	*https://pragprog.com/catalog*
Customer Service:	*support@pragprog.com*
International Rights:	*translations@pragprog.com*
Academic Use:	*academic@pragprog.com*
Write for Us:	*http://write-for-us.pragprog.com*
Or Call:	+1 800-699-7764

Ingram Content Group UK Ltd.
Milton Keynes UK
UKHW031851190623
423702UK00009B/864